Chapter B1

The Open University

First level
disciplinary
course

Using Mathematics

BLOCK B
DISCRETE MODELS

Functions and
calculations

Prepared by the course team

CHAPTER

B1

About this course

This course, MST121 *Using Mathematics*, and the courses MU120 *Open Mathematics* and MS221 *Exploring Mathematics* provide a flexible means of entry to university-level mathematics. Further details may be obtained from the Central Enquiry Service (see address below).

MST121 uses the software program Mathcad (MathSoft, Inc.) and other software to investigate mathematical and statistical concepts and as a tool in problem solving. This software is provided as part of the course, and its use is covered in the associated Computer Book.

The Open University, Walton Hall, Milton Keynes, MK7 6AA.

First published 1997. Reprinted 1998

Edited, designed and typeset by the Open University using the Open University TEX System.

Printed in the United Kingdom by Caligraving Limited, Thetford, Norfolk.

ISBN 0 7492 7840 4

This text forms part of an Open University First Level Course. If you would like a copy of *Studying with The Open University*, please write to the Central Enquiry Service, PO Box 200, The Open University, Walton Hall, Milton Keynes, MK7 6YZ. If you have not already enrolled on the Course and would like to buy this or other Open University material, please write to Open University Educational Enterprises Ltd, 12 Cofferidge Close, Stony Stratford, Milton Keynes, MK11 1BY, United Kingdom.

1.3

Contents

Introduction to Block B   4

Study guide   5

Introduction   6

1   Algebra and machines: conventions and calculations   8
   1.1   Conventions in algebra   8
   1.2   Algorithms   12

2   Investigating Mathcad   21
   2.1   Investigating expressions   21
   2.2   Investigating functions   21

3   Calculations in context   23
   3.1   Functions and calculations   23
   3.2   Editing text on a computer   25
   3.3   Monitoring traffic flows   31

4   Sets and functions   36
   4.1   Expressing sets   36
   4.2   Sets of pairs and triples   38
   4.3   Boolean values   40
   4.4   Characters   42
   4.5   Operations as functions   46

5   Sequences   51
   5.1   Finite sequences   51
   5.2   Functions on sequences   53
   5.3   Adding sequences of numbers   57

6   Expressions and trees   59

7   Editing expressions in Mathcad   67

8   Rules of manipulation   70

Summary of Chapter B1   73
   Learning outcomes   73

Solutions to Activities   75

Solutions to Exercises   78

Introduction to Block B

Block B consists of three chapters:

Chapter B1, *Functions and calculations,*

Chapter B2, *Modelling with sequences,*

Chapter B3, *Modelling with matrices.*

Chapters B2 and B3 develop the theme of modelling introduced in Block A. Chapter B2 considers two models using sequences. These models do not involve any new mathematics, but are explored in some depth. The focus in Chapter B2 centres on the issues involved in setting up, investigating and interpreting models in practice. The chapter concludes with a first look at an important new mathematical idea: *the limit of a sequence.* The concept of limit underlies the ideas of calculus, which is the theme of Block C. Chapter B3 goes on to consider models involving *linked* sequences. For example, suppose that P_n is the number of people who are 14 or under in a population, and Q_n is the number of people who are over 14 (at time n) in the population. Then P_{n+1} will depend on both P_n and Q_n, as will Q_{n+1}. To handle such models, we introduce a new mathematical idea: *matrices.* The chapter looks at both the mathematics of matrices, and at models involving linked sequences.

Chapter B1 has a rather different flavour; it focuses on calculations. You will now have had sufficient experience of Mathcad to be aware that communication with a computer has its own peculiar characteristics. Chapter B1 is not concerned solely with Mathcad, though. It looks at certain general aspects of communicating with computers, and expressing how calculations are to be performed. The chapter concentrates on some particular issues that are both of general relevance in computing, and link to your other mathematical work in the course. Although modelling is not central to Chapter B1, it does consider examples of possible applications where the focus is on expressing what is needed for the application in terms suitable for a computer.

Overall, there are four weeks to study Block B and to complete the associated assessment. Chapter B1 will require about a week and a half, and Chapters B2 and B3 will each require just over a week.

Study guide

Overall this chapter requires about one and a half study weeks; it falls into six study sessions:

Section 1; Section 2; Section 3; Section 4; Section 5; Sections 6–8.

Each session should take about 2 to $2\frac{1}{2}$ hours.

Sections 1, 3, 4, 5 and 8 involve only the printed text. Sections 2 and 7 require use of Mathcad, and Sections 6 and 7 involve use of audio. You can study Section 3 before Section 2 without difficulty. (Section 3 does contain one or two references to Section 2, but these are minor and would not affect your study.) Also, you can study Sections 6–8 before Section 5. These sections do not depend greatly on the material in Sections 3 and 4, but they do use ideas in Subsection 4.5. The recommended study route and an alternative one are indicated on the structural diagram.

If you find it helpful, draw up a planning sheet to schedule your study of this chapter. Remember to include time for work on the computer and for the assignment material. Make sure that you come back to your planning sheet during and at the end of your study of this chapter, to review your progress.

If you have identified areas from your study of Block A on which you want to work further, choose one aspect and concentrate on it in your study of this chapter.

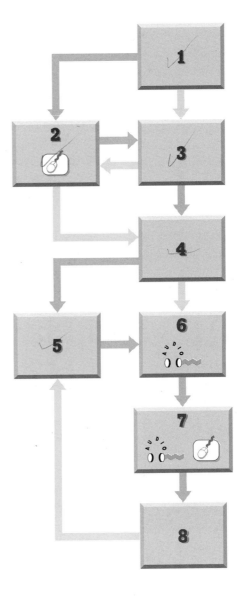

Introduction

One of the major technological advances of recent years has been the development of electronic computers, capable of storing great amounts of information and of very rapid processing. This processing may involve calculations with numbers, but much more often the end result involves other things: perhaps electronic processing of text, or storage and retrieval of information such as addresses or flight times of aeroplanes.

This development of computing has had a significant effect on mathematics. In particular, efficient tools for mathematical calculations, such as Mathcad, have become available. But it also provides a significant new area of study. Admittedly, many aspects of the use of computers fall outside mathematics: for example, the design of effective user interfaces involves understanding of human psychology, and effective production of large pieces of software involves managerial and engineering skills. However, the actual processes that a computer performs are exact calculations, and as such their study is naturally related to mathematics.

The broad aim of this chapter is to provide a first look at the interface between mathematics and computers. A single chapter can do no more than touch the surface of such a broad topic. We shall concentrate on aspects that relate to your other studies in the course. In particular, the chapter has two central themes. One is issues arising from the handling of algebraic expressions by a machine, and, in particular, how Mathcad does this. The other is the way the mathematical concept of function can be used to provide a broad description of a computational process. This process might be one that a machine (and its software) can already perform. Or the computation might be one that you want to enable the computer to perform.

You have now seen several examples of how modelling leads to the need for numerical calculations. Here, we shall concentrate on features relating to how a variety of calculations can be carried out by a machine. These calculations may involve numbers, like those you met in earlier chapters. They may also involve other types of object. For example, a word processor needs to be able to work with sequences of symbols entered from the keyboard ("characters").

Each sort of computer software handles certain *types* of object, and has certain *processes* to manipulate these objects. For example, a computer algebra package handles algebraic expressions, and can evaluate them, solves equations symbolically, and so on. A word-processing package handles text and has processes enabling editing and formatting of this text.

When working with a calculating machine, be it a computer or hand calculator, you need a precise understanding of what instructions it can accept, and how it will interpret them. The machine will interpret any instructions you give it in a quite literal way. Consequently, you need to be very clear about what you want a computer to do. And you need to express your instructions to it precisely, and in terms that the machine can interpret. Modern, "user-friendly", software is designed to make it as easy as possible to achieve what you want, but, even so, these comments remain relevant.

Mathematical ideas can help to clarify calculational processes of all types. The idea of *function* provides a general view of such processes. To express precisely the effect of some process, we need to understand what objects it operates on (its *domain*), what sort of objects it produces (its *codomain*), and its effect (its *rule*). You need to be aware of when processes may fail. For example, division by zero is not defined. Such a "failure" must be reflected in the domain of the function associated with the process of division.

Each model of calculator, or piece of software, has its own individual functionalities. A common feature in designing a method for a calculation is how to obtain "what you want" using "what you have". A detailed set of instructions, showing how to calculate some desired quantity ("what you want") is called an *algorithm*. In an algorithm, the individual instructions need to be expressed in terms of what the machine can already interpret ("what you have"). In Subsection 1.2 you will consider algorithms designed to evaluate simple algebraic expressions. The purpose of that is to introduce some general ideas about designing and expressing algorithms, rather than a concern with how such calculations might be carried out in practice.

The chapter starts by looking at expressions, such as $(3 + 4) \times 7$ or $(x^2 + 1)/(x - 3)$. In writing such expressions in normal mathematical notation, certain conventions are used: for example, $3x$ is interpreted as $3 \times x$. You need to be aware of such conventions when communicating with a machine, which may not use exactly the same conventions and notations as are usual in mathematics.

Section 2 asks you to investigate some aspects of Mathcad, both to develop points from Section 1 and to look ahead to some ideas in later sections. Section 3 looks at two examples of applications, and in particular at how the concept of function can help you to be clear about what is required from a calculation. These applications will probably seem rather different from the modelling examples in earlier chapters. This is because they concern a different aspect of problem solving with mathematics. Previously, you were concerned with obtaining a model involving a mathematical representation to address a "real" problem. Here, the emphasis is not on the modelling required to obtain a mathematical representation, but rather on expressing that representation in terms suitable for a computer.

Sections 4 and 5 are concerned with some mathematical ideas needed here, which are also of wide importance in mathematics: *sets* and *functions*. Section 6 returns to algebraic expressions, and introduces a form of diagram (called a *tree*) that shows how an expression is made up from its component elements. This helps in editing expressions in Mathcad, as you will see in Section 7. Finally, Section 8 looks at properties of numbers that are used in algebraic manipulation.

In this chapter you will meet a number of new technical terms. Some of these are new pieces of standard mathematical terminology, with whose use you will become familiar as you continue your study of mathematics. Others relate to this chapter's discussion of communication with a computer, and are not used much elsewhere in the course. In both cases you need to become familiar with "managing new terminology", and that is the learning skills theme for this chapter.

1 Algebra and machines: conventions and calculations

Mathematical modelling frequently requires you to handle numerical and algebraic expressions. As a simple example, in estimating how much paint you need for a room of length 3.8 m, breadth 2.2 m and height 2.5 m, you might take the area of the walls to be

$$(2.2 + 3.8) \times 2.5 \times 2 \, \mathrm{m}^2$$

(ignoring windows and doors!). An algebraic expression typical of those that arise in modelling is

$$\pi(x^2 - y^2)/t.$$

You have seen in earlier chapters how such expressions arise in modelling (and you will see more in later chapters). Here, however, we shall step aside from the modelling process, and focus attention on such expressions themselves. In particular, we shall concentrate on issues that arise when we consider how a computer may interpret such expressions. Mathcad helps you to handle them: it will, for example, evaluate a purely arithmetic expression, or tabulate the algebraic expression above for various values of x (given values for y and t).

1.1 Conventions in algebra

Successful use of any computer algebra package will require that you communicate effectively with the machine. You need to feed it expressions that are correctly formed, so that it can interpret them. And you want to be sure that the machine will interpret the expression in the way that you intend it to. Let us look at an example.

The numerical expression above reduces to $(2.2 + 3.8) \times 5$; here the brackets tell you that you must first add 2.2 and 3.8, before multiplying the result by 5. Suppose that, in error, you entered this expression into a machine as

$$(2.2 + 3.8 \times 5$$

or even as

$$2.2 + 3.8 \times 5.$$

In the first case, most machines would respond with an error message. Any correctly formulated expression will have the same number of open brackets, '(', as close brackets, ')'. The expression $(2.2 + 3.8 \times 5$ fails this simple check, which is readily built into the software. If one was entirely strict, one would regard the second expression as ambiguous, and you might expect a machine to respond with an error message. After all, does it mean

$$(2.2 + 3.8) \times 5 \quad \text{(do the addition first)}$$

or

$$2.2 + (3.8 \times 5) \quad \text{(do the multiplication first)}?$$

If you do the addition first, you obtain $6.0 \times 5 = 30.0$, but if you do the multiplication first, you obtain $2.2 + 19.0 = 21.2$, so these do not give the same value! In normal mathematical usage, though, we *do* interpret $2.2 + 3.8 \times 5$. It is taken to mean $2.2 + (3.8 \times 5)$, through a convention that gives '×' **precedence** over '+' in the absence of brackets. That is, in an expression containing both these operations, all multiplications are evaluated first, then additions. One would expect such a standard rule of precedence to be built into software handling expressions, so a machine can be expected to interpret $2.2 + 3.8 \times 5$ as meaning $2.2 + (3.8 \times 5)$, rather than responding with an error message. It certainly will not interpret it as $(2.2 + 3.8) \times 5$, so if that is what you intended, all that follows will be wrong!

This may seem to be nothing new, and indeed it is not. If you wrote $2.2 + 3.8 \times 5$ in an assignment answer in error for $(2.2 + 3.8) \times 5$, your tutor would interpret it as $2.2 + (3.8 \times 5)$, just as a machine would. But your tutor would probably pick this up as a minor slip, from its context in the answer as a whole. A machine cannot do that.

Incidentally, there is nothing wrong with including brackets in an expression such as $2.2 + (3.8 \times 5)$. These brackets may not be strictly necessary, given the convention giving × precedence over +. But there is no danger of $2.2 + (3.8 \times 5)$ being misinterpreted.

Activity 1.1 Checking brackets

Is the expression below valid (i.e. correctly formulated)? Explain your answer, briefly.

$$(5 - (3 - 2) \times 4 \times (3 + 7)/6$$

Comment

A solution is given on page 75.

Activity 1.2 Reflecting on precedence

Explain how you would interpret each of the expressions below. In each case, are you using any precedence rules in making your interpretation? Are you sure that your interpretation is standard practice?

(a) $10 - 2 \times 4$

(b) $5 + 6/2$

(c) $5/6 + 2$

(d) $5 \times 2 \times 3$

(e) $5 + 3 - 2$

(f) $10 - 3 + 2$

(g) $4 - 5 - 2$

(h) $40/4/2$

(i) 22π

(j) $\sin 3x + 2$

Comment

(a) I would interpret this as

$$10 - (2 \times 4),$$

which is $10 - 8 = 2$. This interpretation *does* use a precedence rule; the $\times$ has been given precedence over $-$. If there were no precedence, then the expression could also be read as

$$(10 - 2) \times 4,$$

which equals 32.

(b) I would interpret this as

$$5 + (6/2),$$

which is $5 + 3 = 8$, and not as $(5 + 6)/2 = 5\frac{1}{2}$. Again, this interpretation uses a precedence rule; this time giving division precedence over addition.

(c) I would interpret this as $(5/6) + 2$, again giving division precedence over addition.

I would think that both the precedence rules used in (a), (b) and (c) *are* standard practice. However, if I were entering these expressions into a machine, I would include the brackets as a precaution, and use

$$10 - (2 \times 4) \quad \text{for (a),}$$
$$5 + (6/2) \quad \text{for (b),}$$

and

$$(5/6) + 2 \quad \text{for (c).}$$

(d) This time there is no ambiguity. There is a subtle point here for machine interpretation, though. The symbol $\times$ is an instruction to multiply *two* numbers. So does $5 \times 2 \times 3$ mean:

first find 5×2, then multiply this value by 3 (find $(5 \times 2) \times 3$)

or

first find 2×3, then multiply this number by 5 (find $5 \times (2 \times 3)$)?

As it happens, it does not matter which choice is made, since the result is the same either way:

$$(5 \times 2) \times 3 = 10 \times 3 = 30$$

and

$$5 \times (2 \times 3) = 5 \times 6 = 30.$$

But without further programming, the expression $5 \times 2 \times 3$ will appear to be ambiguous to a machine, since it will not know that $(5 \times 2) \times 3$ and $5 \times (2 \times 3)$ will give the same result. A rule allowing interpretation of products like $5 \times 2 \times 3$, involving more than two numbers, will need to be built into the software, just like the precedence rules.

(e) There is no danger of ambiguity in this case, since

$$(5 + 3) - 2 = 5 + (3 - 2).$$

(f) There *is* a potential ambiguity here, since

$$(10 - 3) + 2 = 7 + 2 = 9,$$

whereas

$$10 - (3 + 2) = 10 - 5 = 5.$$

A sample of people that I asked all agreed that they would interpret this expression as

$$(10 - 3) + 2.$$

However, they did not agree as to *why* they gave this interpretation! Some said that "minus" would be given precedence over "plus". Others thought that the expression should be read "from the left", treating each operation as you come to it.

This illustrates why some of my comments here are phrased rather cautiously. Unlike most mathematics, there is no absolute agreement as to exactly what rules are standard in interpreting expressions. There are some that *are* standard, though, and in particular, the rule that brackets say "do this first" is universally accepted. That is why I frequently include brackets as a precaution against misinterpretation.

(g) Here there is again a possible ambiguity, since

$$(4 - 5) - 2 = -1 - 2 = -3,$$

whereas

$$4 - (5 - 2) = 4 - 3 = 1.$$

The most likely interpretation of this is to read from the left, treating the operations as you come to them, and so to read it as $(4 - 5) - 2$. But I should not be confident that this interpretation is entirely standard, and would include brackets here to convey my intention. (We could not even use a rule giving minus precedence over plus to interpret this expression, since that would not tell us which of the two minus operations to treat first.)

(h) This is certainly ambiguous. There are two possible, and different, readings here:

$$(40/4)/2 = 10/2 = 5 \quad \text{or} \quad 40/(4/2) = 40/2 = 20.$$

I do not know how other people would read this one, although it is perhaps more likely for the operations to be read in order from the left, and so for the expression to be interpreted as $(40/4)/2$. Again, I should certainly use brackets here.

(i) I would interpret this as $22 \times \pi$. This involves another convention used in writing algebra, where, for example, "$5y$" is written to mean "five y", that is, $5 \times y$. This convention is extended to writing ab to mean $a \times b$, for example.

This convention is not suitable for use on computers. This is because computers need to distinguish between a situation where, for example, "tan" is the name of the tangent function, and one where "tan" means $t \times a \times n$. So, when using Mathcad, all multiplications need to be entered explicitly.

(j) This is potentially ambiguous. It could be read as $\sin(3x + 2)$ or as $\sin(3x) + 2$ which is not the same. The second interpretation, as $\sin(3x) + 2$, is the likely meaning, giving precedence to calculation of the function sin over addition. But it would be much safer to include brackets, to make the intended meaning quite clear.

Precedence rules are among a number of conventions used in standard mathematical notation. Such conventions reduce the number of symbols needed in expressions, and so may make them easier to read. They are easier to read only if you know the conventions, though! These conventions can cause confusion for a student learning to interpret algebra. This is partly because the conventions are frequently used without being explained. You may find it useful to keep a record in your Learning File of conventions for interpreting algebraic expressions that are used in the course – and whether or not they were explained! If you are not sure what some expression means, this may be a result of a convention of which you are not aware. Check it out with your tutor, or a fellow student. For example, one convention often used is to write the square of $\sin x$ as

$$\sin^2 x.$$

This means the same as $(\sin(x))^2$ (first take the sin, then square the result), but there is no reason why you should know that until it has been explained. (The same convention is used for other trigonometric functions like cos and tan, and for other powers of trigonometric functions.)

Precedence rules allow us to leave out brackets in certain circumstances. However, you do not *have* to leave out such brackets. For example, writing $5 + (6/2)$ gives a helpful reminder to do the division before the addition. A useful rule of thumb when writing down expressions for yourself is: if in doubt, include brackets (and do the bracket counting check). If you are communicating with a machine, and are not sure what precedence rules it may have, then the inclusion of brackets in all cases is the safe course.

1.2 Algorithms

Suppose that you want to know, for example, the value of

$$\pi(6.1^2 - 2.2^2)/0.01.$$

(This is the algebraic expression on page 8 with $x = 6.1$, $y = 2.2$ and $t = 0.01$.) If you are using Mathcad, or a graphics calculator, you can simply enter the expression, and ask for its value. However, if you are working by hand, or using a less sophisticated calculator, you need to do the evaluation as a sequence of steps. You could proceed like this.

Find 6.1^2.	(1)
Find 2.2^2.	(2)
Subtract the result of Line (2) from the result of Line (1).	(3)
Multiply this by π.	(4)
Divide this by 0.01.	(5)

The result of Line (5) is the required value.

An explicit set of instructions which specify how to perform some calculation is called an **algorithm**. The procedure given above is an algorithm, but it is not the only way that we could go about evaluating the given expression. (Lines (4) and (5) could be interchanged, for example.) Typically, for any specified target, there will be several different algorithms to evaluate it.

You would not need to supply an algorithm to enable Mathcad to perform a calculation like this. However, there are many situations where one needs to enable a computer to do a calculation that it cannot yet perform directly. In such a situation, an algorithm is needed. We shall consider some general ideas about algorithms in this familiar context of evaluating an expression. Later in the chapter you will meet some other, new, contexts in which algorithms are required.

In the algorithm above, the various steps find interim values used later in the calculation. Many computer programming languages require you to specify memory locations where any such interim values are to be stored. You might picture a computer as a number of named storage locations, together with a processing area as in Figure 1.1.

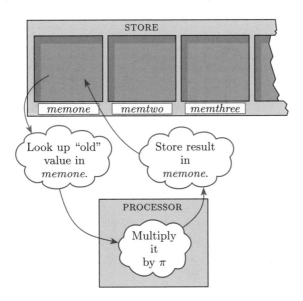

Figure 1.1   Picturing a computer

Suppose we have storage locations named *memone*, *memtwo*, and so on. With references to named storage locations, the algorithm above can be expressed as follows. (Figure 1.1 illustrates Line (4).)

Find 6.1^2, and store this in *memone*. (1)

Find 2.2^2, and store this in *memtwo*. (2)

Subtract the value in *memtwo* from the value in *memone*, and store (3) the result in *memone*.

Multiply the value in *memone* by π, and store the result in *memone*. (4)

Divide the value in *memone* by 0.01, and store the result in *memone*. (5)

The calculated value is in *memone*.

When using memory locations, you must remember that any particular location can hold only one value at a time. So each time you store a value in a particular location, the new value stored replaces any value previously stored (and that previously stored value is lost).

You can check that the above algorithm is doing what you want by keeping track of the various values stored after each step in the algorithm, as in the table below. (Where '−' is shown in the table, no value has yet been stored.) We refer to such a table of intermediate values as a **trace** of the algorithm. Such a trace is useful when checking that the algorithm is correctly designed.

Line	*memone*	*memtwo*
1	6.1^2	−
2	6.1^2	2.2^2
3	$6.1^2 - 2.2^2$	2.2^2
4	$(6.1^2 - 2.2^2) \times \pi$	2.2^2
5	$(6.1^2 - 2.2^2)\pi/0.01$	2.2^2

You can see that after Line (5), *memone* does indeed contain the expression that we wished to calculate. Notice that tracing like this, giving *expressions* at each step, enables you to be sure that the algorithm is going to calculate the desired value. If instead you give the results of the calculation (as decimals) at each step, you will know what value has been calculated, but the tracing process will not tell you whether or not the *correct* value has been found. The actual calculation can be carried out on a machine (if you have access to suitable software).

Activity 1.3   Tracing an algorithm

Trace the expressions stored after each step of the algorithm below. What is the expression whose value is calculated by the algorithm?

Store 10 in *memone*. (1)

Divide the value in *memone* by 4, and store the result in *memtwo*. (2)

Subtract 2 from the value in *memtwo*, and store the result in *memthree*. (3)

Apply the function exp to the value in *memthree*, and store the result in *memthree*. (4)

Multiply the values in *memtwo* and *memthree*, and store the result in *memtwo*. (5)

The calculated value is in *memtwo*.

Comment

A trace is given below.

Line	*memone*	*memtwo*	*memthree*
1	10	–	–
2	10	10/4	–
3	10	10/4	$10/4 - 2$
4	10	10/4	$\exp(10/4 - 2)$
5	10	$(10/4)\exp(10/4 - 2)$	$\exp(10/4 - 2)$

The value calculated is that in *memtwo* after Line (5):

$$(10/4)\exp(10/4 - 2).$$

> You met the exponential function exp in Section 4 of Chapter A4.

The algorithms given above calculate purely numerical expressions, leading to a single value. But suppose that you want an algorithm to evaluate the algebraic expression

$$(y/4)\exp(y/4 - 2),$$

for a general value of y.

The algorithm in Activity 1.3 shows how to find the value of this expression when $y = 10$. For some other value of y, say $y = 2$, the expression will have a different value. But the structure of the expression remains the same, and this means that much of the strategy of calculation in the algorithm can still be used.

Activity 1.4   Generalising

(a) How would you modify the algorithm in Activity 1.3 to evaluate the expression $(y/4)\exp(y/4 - 2)$ for the following cases?

  (i) $y = 2$

  (ii) $y = -3$

  (iii) y takes some general, unspecified, value.

(b) Trace your algorithm when y takes a general value, and show that the correct value is calculated.

Comment

(a) In each case, we need to modify only Line (1) to store the appropriate value in *memone* at the start.

   (i) Store 2 in *memone*. (1)

   (ii) Store -3 in *memone*. (1)

   (iii) Store y in *memone*. (1)

(b) With Line (1) modified as in (a)(iii), we can trace values as below.

Line	*memone*	*memtwo*	*memthree*
1	y	–	–
2	y	$y/4$	–
3	y	$y/4$	$y/4 - 2$
4	y	$y/4$	$\exp(y/4 - 2)$
5	y	$(y/4)\exp(y/4 - 2)$	$\exp(y/4 - 2)$

After Line (5), *memtwo* does contain the value of the required expression.

The algorithm in the comment above shows how we can evaluate the expression $(y/4)\exp(y/4 - 2)$ as a series of steps (for any value of y). Now our purpose here is to introduce some principles that apply to calculational procedures quite generally. In any calculation, your first concern is the quantity you want to find. (In the example in Activity 1.4, it is the value of the given expression.) You then look at what you have available in order to find it. (Be it pen and paper, a hand calculator, or a sophisticated computer algebra package.) In deciding how to calculate the desired quantity, you will certainly take into account what is available. An algorithm to perform the required calculation can be seen as a ladder, enabling you to get from "what you have" to "what you want".

In the context of evaluating algebraic expressions, "what you have" is very different in the case of doing the calculation by hand, as against using Mathcad. To introduce ideas about algorithms, we ask you to imagine that "what you have" is only:

   memory locations (as many as you like);

   the ability to work out the values of standard arithmetic operations (addition, subtraction, multiplication and division) and to find powers (a^b);

   the ability to find values of standard "scientific" functions: sine, exponential, square root, and so on.

In expressing algorithms, it is convenient to have a notation for the instruction "and store the result in". The symbol ":=" is used for this. For example, we write

   $memone := 1$

to mean

   store the value 1 in *memone*.

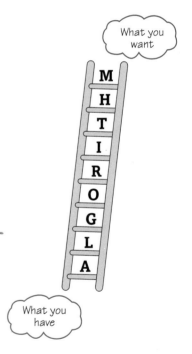

The symbol := is referred to as the **assignment** symbol. You will see how this symbol relates to Mathcad's := in Section 2.

Using this notation, the algorithm in Activity 1.3, with the general version of Line (1) as given in Activity 1.4(a)(iii), can be rewritten in the algebraic shorthand form given below.

$$memone := y \tag{1}$$
$$memtwo := memone/4 \tag{2}$$
$$memthree := memtwo - 2 \tag{3}$$
$$memthree := \exp(memthree) \tag{4}$$
$$memtwo := memtwo \times memthree \tag{5}$$

The calculated value is in *memtwo*.

There are several points to notice here.

◇   The names of storage locations are used to refer to the values stored in them. In the expression to the *right* of the symbol :=, these names refer to the values stored *before* the current instruction is executed. To the *left* of :=, the names refer to the values stored *after* the instruction is executed. For example, Line (4) above says the following.

> Take the value currently stored in *memthree*, and find the exponential of this.
> Store this calculated value in *memthree* (replacing the old value).

◇   The final line in the algorithm tells you *where* the result of the calculation is to be found.

◇   When a computer uses such an algorithm, it will perform the calculation for some particular value of y. But an algorithm is able to express the method of calculation in a *general* way: the same steps, in the same order, are used whatever value y may have.

Activity 1.5   Designing an algorithm

Give an algorithm to evaluate the expression

$$x(\cos(3x - 2))^2 \exp(3x - 2),$$

for a general value of x, where "what you have" is as listed above. First express your instructions in words, then write them algebraically, using the symbol :=. Trace your algorithm for a general value of x, to verify that it calculates the correct quantity.

Comment

There is more than one suitable approach. One possibility is as below.

Store x in *memone*. (1)
Multiply the value in *memone* by 3, and store the result in *memtwo*. (2)
Subtract 2 from the value in *memtwo*, and store the result in *memtwo*. (3)
Apply the function exp to the value in *memtwo*, and store the result in *memthree*. (4)
Apply the function cos to the value in *memtwo*, and store the result in *memfour*. (5)
Square the value in *memfour*, and store the result in *memfour*. (6)
Multiply the values in *memone* and *memfour*, and store the result in *memfour*. (7)
Multiply the values in *memfour* and *memthree*, and store the result in *memfour*. (8)
The calculated value is in *memfour*.

We can express this algebraically as below.

$$memone := x \tag{1}$$
$$memtwo := 3 \times memone \tag{2}$$
$$memtwo := memtwo - 2 \tag{3}$$
$$memthree := \exp(memtwo) \tag{4}$$
$$memfour := \cos(memtwo) \tag{5}$$
$$memfour := memfour^2 \tag{6}$$
$$memfour := memone \times memfour \tag{7}$$
$$memfour := memfour \times memthree \tag{8}$$

The calculated value is in *memfour*.

We can trace the evaluation of this algorithm as below.

Line	memone	memtwo	memthree	memfour
1	x	–	–	–
2	x	$3x$	–	–
3	x	$3x-2$	–	–
4	x	$3x-2$	$\exp(3x-2)$	–
5	x	$3x-2$	$\exp(3x-2)$	$\cos(3x-2)$
6	x	$3x-2$	$\exp(3x-2)$	$(\cos(3x-2))^2$
7	x	$3x-2$	$\exp(3x-2)$	$x(\cos(3x-2))^2$
8	x	$3x-2$	$\exp(3x-2)$	$x(\cos(3x-2))^2 \exp(3x-2)$

The value calculated is in *memfour* after Line (8), and is, as required,

$$x(\cos(3x-2))^2 \exp(3x-2).$$

The algorithm in Activity 1.5 works for any real number x. In the next example, we need to be a little more careful.

Activity 1.6   Watch your step

Trace the algorithm below for a general value of y. What expression is calculated by this algorithm? Are there any values of y for which the calculation will not work?

$$memone := y \tag{1}$$
$$memtwo := memone^2 \tag{2}$$
$$memthree := memtwo - 4 \tag{3}$$
$$memtwo := memtwo/memthree \tag{4}$$

The calculated value is in *memtwo*.

Comment

A trace is given below.

Line	memone	memtwo	memthree
1	y	–	–
2	y	y^2	–
3	y	y^2	y^2-4
4	y	$y^2/(y^2-4)$	y^2-4

The value calculated is in *memtwo* after Line (4), and is

$$y^2/(y^2-4).$$

Suppose that y is 2 or -2. Then y^2-4 will evaluate to 0, and Line (4) will attempt to divide by 0. Division by 0 is not defined, so the calculation will not work in these cases.

The algorithm in Activity 1.6 calculates the value of the expression

$$y^2/(y^2 - 4),$$

for any real value of y *except* when y takes the value 2 or -2 (when the expression $y^2/(y^2 - 4)$ does not have a value). We can capture both this generality and the exceptions by noting that the algorithm evaluates a *function*. The rule for this function is

$$y \longmapsto y^2/(y^2 - 4),$$

and the domain consists of all the real numbers except 2 and -2. Since I am seeking to use the algorithm in as general a way as possible, I have chosen the domain of this function to be as large as possible. We refer to the function

$$y \longmapsto y^2/(y^2 - 4) \quad (y \text{ in } \mathbb{R}, \ y \neq -2, \ y \neq 2)$$

as **the function evaluated by the algorithm** (for the algorithm in Activity 1.6). For any algorithm described for a general input, we talk about "the function evaluated by the algorithm", and take this to have the *largest possible* domain. (That is, the function will have domain consisting of all input values for which the algorithm works.) For example, the algorithm of Activity 1.4(a)(iii) given on page 16 evaluates the function

$$y \longmapsto (y/4) \exp(y/4 - 2) \quad (y \text{ in } \mathbb{R}).$$

Here the domain is $\mathbb{R}$, since that algorithm works for any real number y.

It is possible to give different algorithms to evaluate the same function. For example, you might rewrite $y^2/(y^2 - 4)$ as

$$1/(1 - 4/y^2)$$

by dividing the top and bottom of the expression by y^2, and base an alternative algorithm on this.

Activity 1.7   Check the domain

An algorithm to evaluate the expression

$$1/(1 - 4/y^2),$$

for a general value of y, is given below.

$memone := y$	(1)
$memone := memone^2$	(2)
$memone := 1/memone$	(3)
$memone := memone \times -4$	(4)
$memone := memone + 1$	(5)
$memone := 1/memone$	(6)

The calculated value is in *memone*.

(a) Are there any values for which this calculation fails? What is the domain of the function evaluated by this algorithm?

(b) Can you see any disadvantage to this approach to evaluating

$$y^2/(y^2 - 4)?$$

Comment

(a) The sequence of values stored in *memone* is:

$$y, \quad y^2, \quad 1/y^2, \quad -4/y^2, \quad 1-4/y^2, \quad 1/(1-4/y^2).$$

If $y = 0$, then Line (3) will cause an error. If $y = 2$ or $y = -2$, then $1 - 4/y^2$ is 0, and Line (6) will cause an error. So the algorithm evaluates a function whose domain consists of all the real numbers except -2, 0 and 2.

(b) The expression $y^2/(y^2 - 4)$ is not defined for $y = 2$ or $y = -2$, so we would not expect any method of calculation to work in these cases. However, if $y = 0$, then this expression *is* defined; it has the value 0. The given algorithm is deficient as a way of calculating

$$y^2/(y^2 - 4),$$

since it fails to work if $y = 0$.

A person might be expected to detect and correct the sort of minor problem illustrated in Activity 1.7(b), but a computer certainly will not. A set of instructions for a computer would need to cover every case. To evaluate

$$y^2/(y^2 - 4),$$

one could use the following sort of structure.

If $y = 0$, then the calculated value is 0.

Otherwise (then give the instructions in the statement of Activity 1.7).

Notice the conditional nature of this instruction. The procedure used to determine the required value is different in two cases. Which procedure to use is determined by the "condition"

$$"y = 0",$$

which may be either "true" or "false" (depending on the value of y). A computer needs to be able to handle such conditions; a point that we shall pick up in a later section.

Managing terminology

Like specialist notation, technical language plays a key role in communication in mathematics. Each enables communication to be both concise and precise. But the use of technical language and specialist notation is effective only if both parties are familiar with the language and notation! For example, if you are discussing a problem with your tutor, you may choose to use a mixture of technical terms and everyday language. But if you are explaining something about the course to a neighbour you would probably decide to avoid using technical terms.

Activity 1.8 Managing terminology

In this section you met the terminology

"the function evaluated by an algorithm".

Imagine that you are asked by a fellow student to explain what this means. Think about how you could do that, and record your ideas on Learning File Sheet 1. (You will return to your explanation later.)

Summary of Section 1

In normal mathematical notation, certain conventions are used in writing and interpreting algebraic expressions. Such conventions include some generally accepted precedence rules, such as that giving × precedence over +. They also include the notation $\sin^2 x$, meaning $(\sin(x))^2$. You need to be aware of these conventions if you are to read and write such expressions correctly. When entering expressions into a computer, you need to be alert to which conventions are built into the software. Liberal use of brackets can help to avoid misinterpretation.

An algorithm is a sequence of instructions which specifies how to perform a calculation. You met an algebraic notation for expressing algorithms, involving use of the assignment symbol :=. An algorithm expressed for a general numerical input will evaluate a function, but the domain of this function is not necessarily all real numbers. In designing an algorithm, you need to be aware of the target quantity to be calculated ("what you want") and also of "what you have" on which to base the calculation. To illustrate the principle, calculations in this section dealt with the evaluation of algebraic expressions, where "what you have" is an ability to evaluate the standard arithmetic operations $(+, \times, -, /)$, powers and "scientific" functions such as exp and sin.

Exercises for Section 1

Exercise 1.1

This exercise concerns the expression

$$2x - \cos^3 x.$$

(a) What conventions do you need to use in order to interpret this expression?

(b) Give an algorithm to evaluate this expression. (Express each step using just one of the available operations given in "what you have" on page 15.)

(c) Trace your algorithm for a general input value, to verify that it correctly evaluates the given expression.

Exercise 1.2

Trace the algorithm given below for a general input value y in $\mathbb{R}$. What function is evaluated by this algorithm?

$memone := y$	(1)
$memtwo := memone + 1$	(2)
$memthree := memone - 2$	(3)
$memthree = memthree \times memtwo$	(4)
$memtwo := memtwo + 1$	(5)
$memthree := memtwo/memthree$	(6)

The calculated value is in *memthree*.

2 Investigating Mathcad

This section brings together various activities involving use of your computer. The activities in Subsection 2.1 follow up points in Section 1. Those in Subsection 2.2 are in preparation for work later in the chapter. The story behind the later work here is developed elsewhere in the chapter.

The remainder of this section is based on work with Mathcad, and so is in Computer Book B. For future reference, the summary of the section below gives rather more detail than usual.

2.1 Investigating expressions

Refer to Computer Book B for the work in this subsection.

2.2 Investigating functions

Refer to Computer Book B for the work in this subsection.

Summary of Section 2

In Subsection 2.1 you used Mathcad to follow up various issues introduced in Section 1. In expressions, Mathcad does give $\times$ precedence over $+$ and $-$. However, when entering expressions into Mathcad, use of brackets to avoid ambiguity is advisable. This is particularly true if the expression involves division, or is complicated. If an expression is entered into Mathcad with unequal numbers of open and close brackets, then Mathcad *may* respond with an error message. However, it sometimes responds by *introducing* brackets, to correct the bracket count. There is no guarantee that these brackets will be introduced where you had intended them, so care is needed. If you attempt to evaluate an expression at a value outside its domain, Mathcad will give an error message (either "singularity" or "domain error"). In Mathcad, a sequence of assignments to a particular variable behaves like the algorithms considered in Subsection 1.2.

In Subsection 2.2 you investigated the behaviour of two of Mathcad's built-in functions: angle and if. These will be used as examples later in the chapter, to illustrate some general points about functions. The function $\text{angle}(x, y)$ is defined for any real numbers x and y, so long as x and y are not *both* 0; $\text{angle}(x, y)$ gives the angle (in radians) between the positive x-axis and the line from $(0, 0)$ to (x, y) measured anticlockwise. The function $\text{if}(condition, b, c)$ is defined for any real numbers b and c. Here, *condition* must be a condition that may be true or false (such as $2 = 2$, $2 < 3$ or $5 \geq 9$). The value $\text{if}(condition, b, c)$ is b if *condition* is true, and is c if *condition* is false.

Exercise for Section 2

Exercise 2.1

This exercise does *not* require use of Mathcad.

(a) What is the value of each expression below?

   (i) if$(4 < 3, 7, 2)$

   (ii) if$(3 \geq 3, 5, 6)$

(b) For x in $\mathbb{R}$, the notation $|x|$ is used to mean "the magnitude of x", that is,

$$|x| = \begin{cases} x, & \text{if } x \geq 0, \\ -x, & \text{if } x < 0. \end{cases}$$

For example, $|3.2| = 3.2$, while $|-4.76| = 4.76$.

Using the function if, give an expression whose value is equal to $|x|$.

(c) A function $F : \mathbb{R} \longrightarrow \mathbb{R}$ has the rule below.

$$F(x) = \text{if}(10 - 5x \geq 0, 10 - 5x, 0)$$

   (i) What is the value of $F(0)$, $F(1)$ and $F(3)$?

   (ii) Express the rule for the function F, without using the function if.

3 Calculations in context

So far in this chapter you have been concerned with numbers, but most computer software is concerned with other objects as well as numbers. This leads us to generalise our idea of "calculation", to include the manipulation of types of object other than numbers. This section contains two examples; they are chosen as illustrations of the variety of tasks that software can deal with. They are highly simplified, being designed to give a flavour of some basic principles, and are not intended to describe, for example, how word-processing software operates in practice.

You may wonder why we bother to discuss unrealistically simple applications. Realistic applications, be they models or computer software, are usually complicated. These complications tend to obscure important principles, as well as taking a lot of space in the text and a long time to read. Simplified examples often illustrate the fundamental points more clearly.

In this chapter we are particularly concerned with the role of *functions* in calculations. We start by reviewing relevant points about functions you have met.

3.1 Functions and calculations

In Chapter A4 you met the idea of a function as a process, applied to an input to produce an output.

Figure 3.1

In most of the examples of functions you have seen so far, the input and output are real numbers, and the process is the application of a formula, such as

$$y^2/(y^2 - 4).$$

The domain of a function is the collection of all allowable input values, and you have seen two reasons why the domain of a function may not be all the real numbers. First, a function may be defined by a formula that is not valid for all real numbers. For example, the formula above is not defined if y is 2 or -2. So if F is a function with the rule $F(y) = y^2/(y^2 - 4)$, then F must have $y = 2$ and $y = -2$ excluded from its domain. Secondly, when using a function in modelling, you may choose to restrict the domain to reflect aspects of the situation being modelled. For example, in Section 2 of Chapter A4 a function f with rule $f(x) = 4x^2 - 56x + 96$ and domain the interval $[0, 6]$ was used in the exhibition hall problem. Although the formula $4x^2 - 56x + 96$ is defined for any real number x, the values it gives are not meaningful outside $[0, 6]$ in the context of that model.

In Subsection 1.2 you met some ideas relating functions and calculations. The overall effect of a calculation can be described through "the function evaluated by an algorithm". This function gives the relationship between the input value and the value resulting from the calculation, as well as any necessary restrictions on the input value. Given an algorithm, you can trace it to find what function it evaluates. In practice, however, you would more often be doing the reverse. You would know the target of a calculation: "what you want". This target can equally well be described by a function. For example, in Activity 1.5 you designed an algorithm to evaluate the expression

$$x(\cos(3x-2))^2 \exp(3x-2).$$

This expression is defined for any real number x, so the target of that algorithm can be seen as the evaluation of a function, say G, with domain all real numbers, and rule

$$G(x) = x(\cos(3x-2))^2 \exp(3x-2).$$

In designing an algorithm, you also need to know "what you have". You can again use functions to describe the "tools" that a machine and software make available. In Subsection 1.2 we looked at a situation where the available tools included:

the ability to work out the values of standard arithmetic operations (addition, subtraction, multiplication and division) and to find powers (a^b);

the ability to find values of standard "scientific" functions: sine, exponential, square root, and so on.

For example, finding square roots corresponds to the function

$$x \longmapsto \sqrt{x} \quad (x \text{ in } \mathbb{R}, x \geq 0).$$

The standard arithmetic operations, such as multiplication and addition, can also be seen as functions. This is not obvious, but will be discussed later (in Subsection 4.5). To do this, the idea of function needs to be extended.

We shall broaden the idea in several ways. The remainder of this section discusses functions whose inputs and outputs are objects other than numbers. Also, you will see functions which require more than one input value, like the functions angle and if that you met in Section 2. The mathematical underpinning for these extensions to the idea of function is looked at in Section 4.

So far in this chapter, we have usually been concerned with functions for which the process is given by a formula. But the process for a function need not simply be the application of a formula. For example, we can apply the following process to any real number.

Express the number as a decimal.
Find the first digit in its decimal expansion.

This process can be applied to any real number as input, and produces a number as output; so it defines a function, say F, with domain $\mathbb{R}$ and codomain $\mathbb{R}$. For example:

$F(7/3) = 2 \quad (\text{since } 7/3 = 2.3333\ldots);$
$F(429) = 4;$
$F(\pi) = 3 \quad (\text{since } \pi = 3.1415\ldots).$

This process is not given by a formula! For functions handling objects other than numbers, we shall need to use words rather than a formula to express the process.

3.2 Editing text on a computer

Certain software packages enable text to be typed into a computer and edited (Mathcad has such a facility). As an example, we shall look at a very simple text editor. If you are used to modern word-processing packages you may think that this example is unrealistic; in fact it is not unlike the earliest and most simple forms of text editor for computers.

Imagine an editor that shows on the computer screen the text that you have entered so far. This editor has operations that enable you to:

enter an additional character at the end of this text;

delete the last character displayed.

Figure 3.2 illustrates these two operations. A **character** is a symbol obtained by typing the appropriate key on the keyboard, such as 'a' or 'Q' or ';'. In this chapter we use the convention of enclosing a character in single inverted commas where this is needed for clarity. A sequence of characters forms a "piece of text" which, as here, may be enclosed in double inverted commas for clarity.

Subsection 4.4 discusses characters more fully.

(a)   (b)   (c)

Figure 3.2 Computer screen with (a) some text; (b) a character added to the text in (a); (c) a character deleted from the text in (a)

Suppose you have typed in the text

"tortouse"

in this editor, in error for "tortoise". If the two features above are all that is available, then to correct the 'u' to 'i' you would have to delete back to the 'u', then type 'i', and retype the text "se" even though this had been entered correctly the first time. Now I have used text editors that are as basic as this, but for this example we shall assume that the editor has a couple of other features that can be used to save the correct pieces of text. Suppose it has a facility to store text in a memory, and features that:

clear the memory;

add the last character from the text on the screen to the end of the text in the memory;

delete the last character from the text on the screen;

delete the last character from the text in the memory;

add the last character from the text in the memory to the end of the text on the screen.

With these features, the correct text "se" at the end of the example can be saved to memory, character by character, and then retrieved from memory, character by character. The sequence of operations needed to do this is as follows.

Clear the memory.	(1)
Repeat the operations:	
add the last character (from the text) on the screen to the memory;	(2)
delete the last character from the screen;	(3)
until the offending 'u' is the last character on the screen.	
Delete the last character on the screen.	(4)
Add 'i' to the end of the text on the screen.	(5)
Repeat the operations:	
add the last character of the memory to the screen;	(6)
delete the last character of the memory;	(7)
until there is no text left in the memory.	

Activity 3.1   A word-processing algorithm

(a) Suppose that the above sequence of operations is used to correct "tortouse" to "tortoise". Show in a table: the text on the screen and the text in the memory after each step, and which of Lines (1)–(7) you used each time.

(b) Suppose you want to use a similar sequence of operations to correct the spelling of "toytoise" to "tortoise". What modifications would be needed to the above sequence of instructions?

(c) Suppose you want to insert the missing 'h' to correct "Matcad" to "Mathcad". What modifications to the above sequence of instructions would be needed?

Comment

(a)

Line	Screen	Memory
1	"tortouse"	–
2	"tortouse"	"e"
3	"tortous"	"e"
2	"tortous"	"es"
3	"tortou"	"es"
4	"torto"	"es"
5	"tortoi"	"es"
6	"tortois"	"es"
7	"tortois"	"e"
6	"tortoise"	"e"
7	"tortoise"	" "

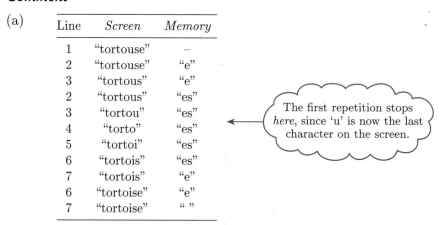

The first repetition stops *here*, since 'u' is now the last character on the screen.

I have used " " to indicate when there is no text stored in memory. The last line in the table will occur, even though it is not needed in order to correct "tortouse", since the instructions say "repeat ... until there is *no text* left in memory".

(b) The reference to 'u' after Line (3) would need to be changed to 'y', and the reference to 'i' in Line (5) changed to 'r'.

(c) The reference to the (offending) 'u' needs to be changed to 't', and the 'i' in Line (5) should be changed to 'h'. Also, Line (4) should be removed.

Now consider these two operations (that we assumed the text editor has):

delete the last character from the text on the screen;
delete the last character from the text in the memory.

These operations are very similar, and each can be seen as an example of a general process:

delete the last character from a piece of text.

In the first operation, this process is applied to "the text on the screen"; in the second operation, it is applied to "the text in the memory". Now the general process is applied to an input, a piece of text, and produces an output that is also a piece of text. So the process "delete the last character" fits our picture of a function. This time, however, the input and output are not numbers, but pieces of text. Some examples of inputs, and the corresponding outputs, are shown in Figure 3.3.

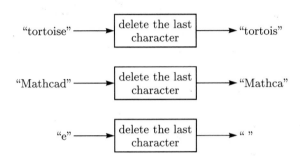

Figure 3.3

We might call this function *DELLAST*. What are the domain and codomain of *DELLAST*? Well, the inputs and outputs are pieces of text, such as "tortoise". If we apply *DELLAST* to a piece of text consisting of just one character, such as "e", we write the resulting output as " ", denoting an **empty** (piece of) text. This empty text, " ", is one possible output from *DELLAST*, and so is in its codomain. However, since " " contains no characters, the process "delete the last character" makes no sense if applied to " " as an *input*, and so we do not include " " in the domain of *DELLAST*. Hence the domain of *DELLAST* is all *non-empty* pieces of text, and its codomain is all pieces of text. Thus

DELLAST inputs a non-empty piece of text, and outputs the piece of text formed by deleting the last character of the input text.

The usual sort of notation can be used to show the application of the function *DELLAST* to a particular input value. We write, for example,

DELLAST("tortoise") = "tortois".

In the algorithm given earlier, to correct the spelling of "tortouse", both "the screen" and "the memory" are used as memory locations. In Section 1 we used named memory locations that could store numbers. I shall now assume that we have memory locations that can also store objects of other types (in particular, pieces of text). Here, I shall write *screen* and *memory* for the memory locations "the screen" and "the memory". Then, using *DELLAST* and the assignment symbol :=, we can express the instruction

delete the last character from the text on the screen,

in the style of Subsection 1.2, as

screen := *DELLAST*(*screen*).

Recall that in this context the names of storage locations are used to refer to the values in them (see the first ◇ on page 16).

To express the other operations in that algorithm in a similar way, we need two other functions. I shall call these *LAST* and *ADDLAST*. They act as follows.

LAST inputs a piece of text, and outputs the last character in that piece of text.

ADDLAST requires two inputs, a character and a piece of text, and outputs the piece of text formed by adding the character to the end of the piece of text.

In describing *ADDLAST*, the word "adding" is used simply in its ordinary English sense (of "append" or "incorporate"). It does not refer to addition (+) of numbers!

So, for example, we have the following.

$LAST(\text{"tortoise"}) = \text{'e'}$

$ADDLAST(\text{'e'}, \text{"bit"}) = \text{"bite"}$

The function *ADDLAST* has two inputs. You have met other functions with more than one input: for example, in Section 2, you met the Mathcad functions angle(x, y), with two inputs, and if$(condition, b, c)$, which has three. We shall discuss in Section 4 how the domains of such functions may be expressed. We can again use a process box to picture the action of the function *ADDLAST*, but this time we need to show two inputs. We can illustrate particular inputs as in Figure 3.4.

Figure 3.4

Or we can picture the action of *ADDLAST* on general inputs as in Figure 3.5.

Figure 3.5

When writing $ADDLAST(c, s)$, we shall always require that the character comes first, then the piece of text. So, for example, $ADDLAST(\text{"bit"}, \text{'e'})$ is not defined, since the inputs are written in the incorrect order.

Activity 3.2   Practice with LAST, ADDLAST and DELLAST

(a) Evaluate:

  (i) $ADDLAST(\text{'s'}, \text{"bee"})$;

  (ii) $LAST(\text{"toytoi"})$.

(b) Suppose an algorithm contains the instruction

  $screen := DELLAST(memory)$,

  where *screen* is "the text shown on the screen", and *memory* is "the text in the memory". Describe in words the effect of this instruction.

(c) Suggest an appropriate domain and codomain for the function *LAST*.

domain - all non-empty pieces of text
codomain - all characters used in forming each piece of text.

Comment

A solution is given on page 75.

We can use the functions $DELLAST$, $LAST$ and $ADDLAST$ to express algebraically algorithms involving text editing. To do this, we may sometimes use combinations of these functions. For example,

$ADDLAST(LAST(\text{"toyt"}), \text{"esio"})$

means "first find the last character of "toyt", and then use this as the first input to $ADDLAST$, with "esio" as the second input. This is shown diagrammatically below.

To evaluate such an expression, we use two steps, first working out $LAST(\text{"toyt"})$, as shown below.

$ADDLAST(LAST(\text{"toyt"}), \text{"esio"})$

$= ADDLAST(\text{'t'}, \text{"esio"})$

$= \text{"esiot"}$

Activity 3.3   Interpreting and expressing instructions

(a) (i) What is the value of the expression below when $screen = \text{"Matc"}$ and $memory = \text{"da"}$?

$ADDLAST(LAST(screen), memory)$

(ii) Express in words the meaning of the instruction below in general, when $memory$ and $screen$ may contain arbitrary pieces of text.

$memory := ADDLAST(LAST(screen), memory)$

Are there any values of $screen$ or of $memory$, for which this instruction could not be executed?

(b) Using the functions $DELLAST$, $LAST$ and $ADDLAST$, assignment, and memory locations $screen$ and $memory$, express algebraically each of the following instructions.

(i) Delete the last character of the text on the screen.

(ii) Add 'i' to the end of the text on the screen.

Comment

(a) (i) Working in two steps, we have

$ADDLAST(LAST(\text{"Matc"}), \text{"da"}) = ADDLAST(\text{'c'}, \text{"da"}) = \text{"dac"}.$

(ii) The value $ADDLAST(LAST(screen), memory)$ expresses the result of taking the last character of the text on the screen, and adding this to the end of the text in the memory. The full instruction tells the computer to replace the old text stored in $memory$ with this new text. The overall effect can be expressed as

add the last character of the text on the screen to the end of the text in the memory.

This instruction could not be executed if the text on the screen is empty, since the empty text " " is not in the domain of $LAST$.

(b) You need to think about two things: how to use the functions to express the particular pieces of text you want, in terms of their old values in *screen* and *memory*; and also, where these new values are to be stored (in *screen* or in *memory*).

(i) *DELLAST*(*screen*) expresses the text obtained by deleting the last character currently on the screen. The given instruction

delete the last character on the screen

suggests that the current text on the screen should be replaced by the text formed by deleting its last character. This is expressed algebraically as

$$screen := DELLAST(screen).$$

(ii) *ADDLAST*('i', *screen*) is the text formed by adding the character 'i' to the end of the current text on the screen. The given instruction suggests that this should become the new text on the screen, so you need

$$screen := ADDLAST('i', screen).$$

On page 26, I gave an algorithm to correct "tortouse" to "tortoise". There, I expressed the algorithm in ordinary language. Now, using assignment, and the functions *DELLAST*, *LAST* and *ADDLAST*, you can express Lines (2)–(7) algebraically. Also, Line (1)

clear the memory

can be expressed as

$$memory := \text{“ ”}.$$

(This ensures that, after Line (1) has been executed, the memory contains an "empty" piece of text.)

As well as the instructions in Lines (1)–(7), the algorithm has another important feature, repetition. In expressing algorithms algebraically, I shall use the format below to indicate when instructions are to be repeated.

Repeat the instructions:
(*instructions*);
until (*condition*).

Most computer programming languages have some structure like this, allowing you to specify that certain instructions are to be repeated. (The exact format varies between languages.) Notice that

the repetition continues until a specified condition becomes true.

Such conditions can also be expressed algebraically (if the necessary functions are available). For example, the condition

there is no text in memory

can be expressed as

$$memory = \text{“ ”}.$$

Notice that this involves equality as a condition, which is why I wrote "=" above, meaning "is equal to". Despite the similar appearance of the symbols = and :=, = has quite a different meaning from := which means "is given the value". (Mathcad makes a similar distinction, and in Activity 2.9 you needed to form such conditions in Mathcad to express

"=" means "is equal to"
":=" means "is given the value".

if($y = 2, 5, 7$), for example.) As well as conditions to terminate repetition, conditions are needed in algorithms to determine which option to use when there is more than one choice (as indicated after the comment to Activity 1.7).

Activity 3.4 Expressing a condition

Using the functions $DELLAST$, $LAST$ and $ADDLAST$ (as needed), and equality, express algebraically the condition

'u' is the last character on the screen.

Comment

A solution is given on page 75.

Activity 3.5 Expressing a complete algorithm

Using the functions $DELLAST$, $LAST$ and $ADDLAST$, assignment, and memory locations *screen* and *memory*, express algebraically the algorithm given on page 26, which corrects "tortouse" to "tortoise".

Comment

A solution is given on page 75.

3.3 Monitoring traffic flows

Many computer applications concern numbers. But they may involve processing numbers in surprising ways. For example, consider a device that counts vehicles passing over it. Suppose that it generates a count of the vehicles passing in each 5 minute period. These counts are stored by a computer as a sequence of numbers, such as

5, 17, 9, ..., 167, 88, 154   (in that order).

Suppose that each count is appended to the end of the sequence as it is recorded, so that 154 is the most recent count in the example above.

Activity 3.6 Recording the counts

Describe (in words) a function that could be used to keep the record of counts up to date.

Comment

As each new count is recorded, it needs to be included at the end of the sequence of counts already stored. To do this, we could use a function with two inputs: a number (the new count) and a sequence of numbers (the old record). The function would output the sequence formed by adding (i.e. appending) the input number to the end of the input sequence.

The function described in the comment above is very similar to the function $ADDLAST$ introduced in Subsection 3.2. You can think of a piece of text, such as "tortoise", as a sequence of characters:

't', 'o', 'r', 't', 'o', 'i', 's', 'e'   (in that order).

Then $ADDLAST$, like the function in the comment above, adds an item at the end of a sequence, but the type of item in the sequence differs in the two cases. In the comment above, the function involves sequences of numbers, whereas the function in Subsection 3.2 involved sequences of characters. Rather than introduce functions with similar actions, but acting on sequences containing different types of object, I shall generalise the definition of $ADDLAST$. I shall assume that $ADDLAST$ will add an item at the end of a sequence, whatever type of item the sequence may contain. So, for example,

$$ADDLAST(5, \langle 2, 4, 1, 3 \rangle) = \langle 2, 4, 1, 3, 5 \rangle.$$

In the equation above, angle brackets $\langle \rangle$ have been used to show that $\langle 2, 4, 1, 3 \rangle$ and $\langle 2, 4, 1, 3, 5 \rangle$ form sequences. We shall continue to use this notation for sequences later, even when the items in the sequence are not numbers.

Suppose that this counting device is to be used to monitor traffic approaching road junctions that it is thought may need to be redesigned. For any given junction, traffic engineers can specify its current capacity – a maximum number of vehicles that it can comfortably handle in 5 minutes with its present design. To determine priorities, various road junctions are being monitored, and the traffic that they are handling is compared with their current capacity. Each junction will be monitored for a week and the record of traffic counts will be used to determine how often its capacity is exceeded. Priority for redesign will be given to the junction whose capacity is exceeded most often (that is, in the greatest number of 5 minute periods).

Activity 3.7   The target function

Think about "what you want" in deciding how often the capacity of a road junction has been exceeded. Could this be described as a function? This function should apply to information about any of the road junctions that have been monitored for a week. What would the function input, and what would it output?

Comment

The function would have the sequence of numbers giving the vehicle counts at the road junction during the week as one input. The function will need a second input. That will be a single number, giving the capacity of the particular road junction.

So "what you want" can be described as a function. That function will have two inputs: a single number, say x, and a sequence of numbers, say s. In fact, s is a sequence of $7 \times 24 \times 12 = 2016$ whole numbers. The function will output a number that gives a count of how many entries in the sequence s exceed x.

We happen to know the number of items in the input sequence for the function described in the preceding comment. However, it is just as easy to design an algorithm to calculate a more general function that will accept any sequence of numbers as input. So, for any number x and for any sequence of numbers s let $COUNTOVER(x, s)$ be the count of how many entries in s are greater than x. For example,

$$COUNTOVER(100, \langle 105, 102, 101, 100, 99, 101 \rangle) = 4,$$

since the sequence $\langle 105, 102, 101, 100, 99, 101 \rangle$ contains four numbers (105, 102, 101, and 101 again) that are greater than 100.

An algorithm to calculate $COUNTOVER$ will require some functions that handle sequences of numbers. Suppose that you have the equivalents for sequences of numbers of all the functions on sequences of characters that were described in Subsection 3.2. So, as with $ADDLAST$, assume that $LAST$ and $DELLAST$ also apply to sequences of numbers as well as to sequences of characters.

How then might you calculate the function $COUNTOVER$ using "what you have", which we shall take to be the functions $LAST$, $ADDLAST$ and $DELLAST$, together with operations on numbers? This can be done by examining the numbers in the input sequence one at a time, using a strategy such as that below. This algorithm uses memory locations seq and num. It finds $COUNTOVER(n, s)$, where n is a number and s is a sequence of numbers.

> Store the input sequence s in seq.
> Store 0 in num.
> Repeat the operations:
> > if the last number in seq is greater than the input number n,
> > then add 1 to num;
> > delete the last number in seq;
> until seq contains no elements.
> The calculated value is in num.

Activity 3.8   Expressing the algorithm for COUNTOVER

Using the functions $LAST$ and $DELLAST$, and operations on numbers, express algebraically each of the following.

(a) (i) The condition

the last number in seq is greater than the input number n.

  (ii) The instruction

delete the last number in seq.

(b) The complete algorithm to evaluate $COUNTOVER(n, s)$. (Use $\langle \rangle$ to denote the empty sequence.)

Comment

(a) (i) The last number in the sequence *seq* is $LAST(seq)$. So this condition is

$$LAST(seq) > n.$$

(ii) If you delete the last number in *seq*, you obtain the sequence $DELLAST(seq)$. The given instruction suggests that the old sequence stored in *seq* should be replaced by $DELLAST(seq)$, and so the instruction can be expressed as

$$seq := DELLAST(seq).$$

(b) The complete algorithm can be expressed algebraically like this.

$seq := s$
$num := 0$
Repeat the instructions:
    if $LAST(seq) > n$ then $num := num + 1$;
    $seq := DELLAST(seq)$;
until $seq = \langle\,\rangle$.
The calculated value is in *num*.

Annotating your Handbook

The next activity invites you to think about how you might annotate an entry in your *Handbook*.

Activity 3.9 Experimenting with annotation

The terminology "the function evaluated by an algorithm" was introduced earlier in the chapter, and you may not recall exactly what it means. Look it up in the *Handbook*, and compare the entry there with your explanation of the term on Learning File Sheet 1 (associated with Activity 1.8). What is helpful (or unhelpful) about each? How might you annotate the *Handbook* entry? Add any annotation that you think might be helpful, in pencil, to your *Handbook*, and record your annotation on Learning File Sheet 1. (If you do not feel that you want to annotate that *Handbook* entry, or you cannot see how to do so in any useful way, leave this activity for now. There is another activity inviting you to think about annotation at the end of the next section.)

Summary of Section 3

Functions can be used to describe "what you want" and "what you have" in a calculation. Two examples were considered here: making corrections using a crude text editor, and processing information (about traffic flows) stored in a sequence of numbers.

A format for expressing repetition in algorithms was introduced. We write the following to indicate that the given instructions are to be repeated until the condition becomes true.

Repeat the instructions:
(*instructions*);
until (*condition*).

Exercise for Section 3

Exercise 3.1

The algorithm below has an input t that is a general piece of text. It uses memory locations *screen* and *count*.

$screen := t$	(1)
$count := 3$	(2)
Repeat the instructions:	
$screen := DELLAST(screen)$	(3)
$count := count - 1$	(4)
until $count = 0$.	

The calculated value is in *screen*.

(a) Trace the values taken by *screen* and *count* when the text $t =$ "boiled" is input. Show which line in the algorithm is used at each step in your trace. What value is output in this case?

(b) What value would you expect the algorithm to calculate when a general piece of text is input?

(c) Are there any values of the input text t for which the algorithm will fail?

(d) Suggest a description of the function evaluated by this algorithm.

4 Sets and functions

The domain of any function is a collection of objects. For example, you have met a function whose domain is

all real numbers except 2 and -2,

and another whose domain is

all non-empty pieces of text.

Any collection of objects, such as these, is called a **set**. Earlier in the chapter, we have used words to describe sets. Here, you will meet a mathematical notation for them.

One of the great strengths of mathematics is its algebraic notation. This notation has the advantages of being concise and precise. At first, its conciseness may make it less easy to read than words, but, with familiarity, it becomes clearer. And imagine trying to express complicated calculations without algebraic notation!

4.1 Expressing sets

One simple way to describe a set is just to list its members. Suppose that $DAYS$ is the set of days of the week. Then we can write

$DAYS = \{$Monday, Tuesday, Wednesday, Thursday, Friday, Saturday,
Sunday$\}$.

The curly brackets tell you that $DAYS$ is a set. Here, the members of the set are listed explicitly within the curly brackets. It is not always possible to list all the members of a set in this way. Recall that the set of all real numbers is written as $\mathbb{R}$. You could not list the members of $\mathbb{R}$. We extend the curly bracket notation to express sets containing "some" real numbers. For example, the set of "all real numbers except 2 and -2" is written

$\{x \in \mathbb{R} : x \neq 2, x \neq -2\}$.

The outer curly brackets show that this is a set. The $x \in \mathbb{R}$ indicates that the set consists of real numbers, and the members of the set are those real numbers that satisfy the condition given after the colon. (That is, the set contains those real numbers that are not 2 or -2.) Similarly, we would write the set of non-negative real numbers as below.

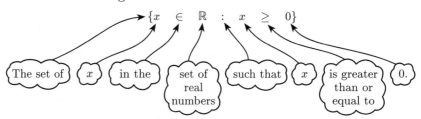

The clouds show how each individual symbol in this notation can be read. However, such a literal reading can lead to clumsy language. You can express this set more clearly as below.

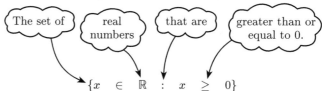

36

The same notation can be used for sets of objects of other types. Suppose **C** is the set of all characters. Then

$\{c \in \mathbf{C} : c$ is a lower-case letter$\}$

C is defined more precisely in Subsection 4.4.

is the set of characters that are lower-case letters. In Chapter A4 you met the notation $\mathbb{N}$ for the set of natural numbers. (Recall that $\mathbb{N}^*$ consists of the natural numbers and 0, that is, $\mathbb{N}^* = \{0, 1, 2, \ldots\}$.) So the set

$\{x \in \mathbb{N} : 5 < x\}$

is the set of natural numbers that are greater than 5. Notice that 8.37, for example, is *not* in this set, since it is not a natural number, though 8.37 *is* in the set $\{x \in \mathbb{R} : 5 < x\}$.

The symbol $\in$ is used more generally to denote when an object is in a particular set. For example, let X be the set

$X = \{n \in \mathbb{N} : 1 \leq n \leq 15\}.$

Then 2 is in X, and we write

$2 \in X.$

However, 17 is not in X, since $17 \leq 15$ is not true. So $17 \in X$ is false. This is usually written as

$17 \notin X.$

In this context $\in$ is read as "is in" or "is a member of", and $\notin$ is read as "is not in" or "is not a member of".

Activity 4.1   Interpreting set notation

(a) Describe in words the set X, where

$X = \{x \in \mathbb{N} : 4 \leq x \leq 20, x \neq 10\}.$

(b) With the set X as in (a), say whether each of the following statements is true or false.

(i) $22 \in X$ ✗

(ii) $15 \in X$ ✓

(iii) $7.23 \in X$ ✗

(c) Let *MONTHS* be the set of months of the year. Write out the set *MONTHS* using curly bracket notation.

(d) (i) Express the set of real numbers between $-\pi/2$ and $\pi/2$ (*not* including $-\pi/2$ or $\pi/2$) using curly bracket notation. $\{x \in \mathbb{R} : \frac{\pi}{2} < x < \frac{\pi}{2}\}$

(ii) In Chapter A4 you met a notation for intervals in $\mathbb{R}$; for example, $[0, 6]$ means the set of real numbers between 0 and 6 *inclusive*. Express the set $[0, 6]$ using curly bracket notation. $\{x \in \mathbb{R} : 0 \leq x \leq 6\}$

Comment

Solutions are given on page 75.

4.2 Sets of pairs and triples

Some of the functions you have met have more than one input. For example, the Mathcad function angle(x, y) inputs two real numbers x and y (where x and y must not both be 0). To express the domain of such a function in curly bracket notation we need a new piece of notation.

As an example of this new notation, imagine that you are designing a program to enable people to play patience on a computer. A basic step in the design is to represent the set of cards in a pack. Now an individual card might be the Jack of diamonds, or the 7 of spades. It is natural to look for a representation that shows these two aspects of a card: its value (Jack or 7, for example), and its suit (diamonds or spades, for example). To achieve this, one might choose to represent a card as a pair $(value, suit)$, where $value$ comes from the set of possible values

$$VALUES = \{2, 3, 4, 5, 6, 7, 8, 9, 10, \text{Jack}, \text{Queen}, \text{King}, \text{Ace}\},$$

and $suit$ comes from the set of possible suits

$$SUITS = \{\text{clubs}, \text{hearts}, \text{diamonds}, \text{spades}\}.$$

We write the set that consists of all the pairs

$$(value, suit),$$

where $value$ is from $VALUES$ and $suit$ is from $SUITS$, as

$$VALUES \times SUITS.$$

Here, the symbol $\times$ has nothing to do with multiplying numbers! This $\times$ is used to denote the set formed by taking pairs in this way.

Using $\times$, we can express the domain of the Mathcad function angle as

$$\{(x, y) \in \mathbb{R} \times \mathbb{R} : x \text{ and } y \text{ are not both } 0\}.$$

This is the set $\mathbb{R} \times \mathbb{R}$ with $(0, 0)$ removed.

In Chapter A3 you were concerned with geometric objects in the plane, such as straight lines and circles. Each such geometric object can be seen as a set of points in the plane, and so can be written using curly bracket notation. For example, the straight line with equation $y = 2x$ is the set

$$\{(x, y) \in \mathbb{R} \times \mathbb{R} : y = 2x\}.$$

Other shapes may need more complicated set descriptions. For example, a square with corners at $(0, 0)$, $(0, 1)$, $(1, 1)$ and $(1, 0)$ forms the set

$$\{(x, y) \in \mathbb{R} \times \mathbb{R} : y = 0 \text{ and } 0 \leq x \leq 1,$$
$$\text{or } y = 1 \text{ and } 0 \leq x \leq 1,$$
$$\text{or } x = 0 \text{ and } 0 \leq y \leq 1,$$
$$\text{or } x = 1 \text{ and } 0 \leq y \leq 1\}.$$

Figure 4.1   A square with corners at $(0, 0)$, $(0, 1)$, $(1, 1)$, $(1, 0)$ forms a set of points in $\mathbb{R} \times \mathbb{R}$

For any sets X and Y, we write $X \times Y$ to mean the set of all pairs (x, y), where x is in X and y is in Y. The order in which we write the sets in the $X \times Y$ notation matters. The set

VALUES × SUITS

contains pairs in the order

(value, suit).

The set

SUITS × VALUES

contains pairs in the reverse order

(suit, value),

and is different from VALUES × SUITS. The order within a pair matters: for example, the pairs $(3, 1)$ and $(1, 3)$ in $\mathbb{R} \times \mathbb{R}$ correspond to different points in the plane.

Some functions have more than two inputs, and to express their domains we extend this notation further. Let **B** be the set {true, false}, representing the values that some condition may take. Then the set $\mathbf{B} \times \mathbb{R} \times \mathbb{R}$ consists of all triples

(b, x, y),

where b is true or false, and each of x and y is a real number. So (true, 1, 0) is a member of $\mathbf{B} \times \mathbb{R} \times \mathbb{R}$, but (1, true, 0) is not because, for example, the first member of the triple is not in **B**.

In Subsection 4.3 you will meet a function which has domain $\mathbf{B} \times \mathbb{R} \times \mathbb{R}$.

Activity 4.2   Sets of pairs and triples

(a) Which of the following are members of the set

$$\{(x, y) \in \mathbb{R} \times \mathbb{R} : x \neq 0\}?$$

(i) $(2.3, -5.1)$ ✓

(ii) $(0, 2)$ ✗

(iii) $(4, 0)$ ✓

(b) Which of the following are members of the set $\mathbf{B} \times \mathbb{R} \times \mathbb{R}$, where $\mathbf{B} = \{\text{true}, \text{false}\}$?

(i) (true, 5, −1.3) ✓

(ii) (false, 0, 0) ✓

(iii) (0, false, 5) ✗

(iv) (true, 5) ✗

Explain how you arrive at your answer.

(c) Let DATESIN97 be the set of dates in the year 1997. Suppose that these dates are represented as pairs (n, m), where n is a natural number and m comes from the set MONTHS described in Activity 4.1(c). Express DATESIN97 algebraically, using the $X \times Y$ and curly bracket notations. $\{(n,m) \in \mathbb{N} \times M :$

(d) In Subsection 2.2 of Chapter A3 we defined a circle of radius r to be the set of points in the plane with coordinates (x, y) such that x squared plus y squared is equal to r squared. Write this set of points using curly bracket notation.

$\{(x,y) \in \mathbb{R} \times \mathbb{R} :$

Comment

Solutions are given on page 75.

4.3 Boolean values

A computer frequently uses the result of some condition to determine what action to perform. The action might, for example, be to decide which choice to make within a list of cases, such as those in the solution to Activity 4.2(c), or to decide when a repetition should stop (as, for example, in the algorithms in Subsections 3.2 and 3.3). Examples of conditions include

whether or not two real numbers are equal;

whether or not two characters are the same;

whether or not a real number is larger than 2.

Consider the condition $x > 2$, where x is a real number. Depending on the value of x, there are two possible outcomes, as demonstrated by

$2.5 > 2$ and $1.3 > 2$.

The first of these statements is true, but the second is not. For such a condition, these are the only two possible values: true and false (meaning "not true"). These are known as **Boolean values**. The set **B** of Boolean values is

$$\mathbf{B} = \{\text{true}, \text{false}\}.$$

> George Boole (1815–1864) was a self-taught mathematician and logician. He laid the foundations of the study of symbolic logic in a book published in 1854. As a young man he taught in schools in Lincoln (his birthplace). In 1849 he was appointed Professor of Mathematics at Queen's College, Cork, and held this post until his death.

Computers handle many functions whose domains or codomains involve the set **B**. For example, consider a function H, whose input is the real number x and whose output is the value of the condition $x > 2$. Then H has domain $\mathbb{R}$ and codomain **B**. As in Chapter A4, we write $H : \mathbb{R} \longrightarrow \mathbf{B}$ to show the domain and codomain of this function.

We refer to a statement of the domain and codomain of any function as its **signature**. Thus the signature of H is $\mathbb{R} \longrightarrow \mathbf{B}$.

As another example, consider the condition $x > y$ comparing *any* two real numbers x and y. Call the function corresponding to this test *GREATER*. Then *GREATER* will require two real numbers as inputs. We shall write a typical input as (x, y). Then, for example, *GREATER*$(5, 4)$ will be true, since $5 > 4$ is true, and *GREATER*$(2, 4.7)$ will be false, since $2 > 4.7$ is false. The function *GREATER* has any pair of real numbers as input and outputs a Boolean value, so the signature of *GREATER* is $\mathbb{R} \times \mathbb{R} \longrightarrow \mathbf{B}$.

Below, the lower clouds show how you can read the symbolism used for giving the signature of a function.

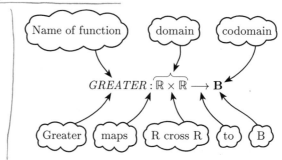

You have used equality as a condition, for example in forming an input for the Mathcad function if. Such comparison of two real numbers to see whether or not they are equal corresponds to a function, say *EQUALNO*, with signature $\mathbb{R} \times \mathbb{R} \longrightarrow \mathbf{B}$.

It is convenient when expressing conditions to have some functions that process Boolean values. Consider, for example, the condition

x is not 2 or -2,

where x is a real number. Suppose we have available a function that determines whether or not two real numbers are equal (so that we can use $=$ in conditions). We can use that to express "x is not 2" if we also have available a function *NOT*, that reverses a Boolean value. That is, *NOT* has domain $\mathbf{B}$, and

$$\begin{vmatrix} NOT(\text{true}) = \text{false}, \\ NOT(\text{false}) = \text{true}. \end{vmatrix}$$

What is more, we can express the original condition in full if we have a further function *AND*, that combines Boolean values as

$$\begin{vmatrix} AND(\text{true}, \text{true}) = \text{true}, \\ AND(\text{true}, \text{false}) = \text{false}, \\ AND(\text{false}, \text{true}) = \text{false}, \\ AND(\text{false}, \text{false}) = \text{false}. \end{vmatrix}$$

Notice that this function gives $AND(a, b)$ as true only when a and b are both true, corresponding to the usual meaning of "and" in English. With these two functions and $=$ available, the original condition "x is not 2 or -2" can be expressed as

$$AND(NOT(x = 2), NOT(x = -2)).$$

Moreover, each of *NOT*, *AND* and $=$ corresponds to an operation that a computer can be expected to have available.

Activity 4.3   Signatures of functions

What is the signature of each of the following functions?

(a) *NOT*

(b) *AND*

Comment

(a) *NOT* has domain $\mathbf{B}$. Its output is also a Boolean value. So its signature is $\mathbf{B} \longrightarrow \mathbf{B}$.

(b) *AND* has two Boolean values as inputs, so its domain is $\mathbf{B} \times \mathbf{B}$. Its output is a Boolean value. So *AND* has signature $\mathbf{B} \times \mathbf{B} \longrightarrow \mathbf{B}$.

Activity 4.4   Expressing conditions algebraically

Using the functions AND and NOT, $=$ and $\leq$ comparing real numbers, express algebraically each of the conditions below on a real number x.

(a) x lies between 4 and 20, inclusive.

(b) x is greater than or equal to 1, but is not equal to 2.

(c) x lies between 4 and 20, inclusive, but is not 10.

Comment

(a) Here x must satisfy each of the two conditions $4 \leq x$ and $x \leq 20$. The combined condition can be expressed using AND, as

$$AND(4 \leq x, x \leq 20).$$

(b) Here x must satisfy each of the two conditions $1 \leq x$ and $x \neq 2$. The second condition can be expressed as $NOT(x = 2)$. Then the two conditions can be combined using AND, as

$$AND(1 \leq x, NOT(x = 2)).$$

(c) This time x must satisfy the condition in (a), and also $x \neq 10$. So you need to combine the condition from (a) with the condition $NOT(x = 10)$ using AND. This gives

$$AND(AND(4 \leq x, x \leq 20), NOT(x = 10)).$$

An alternative, less awkward, way of writing conditions combined using AND is mentioned in Subsection 4.5.

Mathcad represents true as 0, and false as 1.

The Mathcad function if, that you met in Section 2, has a condition as its first input. Unlike much software, Mathcad does not handle Boolean values directly. Instead, it represents true and false using numbers. This is a feature of Mathcad that we do not need to pursue further. In a situation where Boolean values are available, the Mathcad function if corresponds to a function which I shall call IF, with signature $\mathbf{B} \times \mathbb{R} \times \mathbb{R} \longrightarrow \mathbb{R}$, where

$$IF(b, x, y) = \begin{cases} x, & \text{if } b = \text{ true}, \\ y, & \text{if } b = \text{ false}. \end{cases}$$

4.4   Characters

If you use word-processing software on a computer, the result of pressing a key on the keyboard is usually that the corresponding symbol appears on the screen. The sequence of the symbols you type gradually produces the text you want. Not every key (or key combination) has the straightforward effect of producing a symbol, of course. Some are used to control the layout of text: to separate paragraphs, to indent text, or to format symbols as italic or bold, for example. Others are used to control the software itself (saving, quitting, and so on). Here, we shall be concerned simply with the symbols that can appear on the screen (and may later be printed), rather than with these other processes.

An individual symbol is called a **character**. For example, 'a', 'A' and ';' are characters, produced on the screen by pressing the appropriate key. In this context we distinguish upper-case and lower-case letters: 'Q' and 'q' are *different* characters. They are just as different as, say '(' and '9', which are also produced by the same key, with and without the shift key also being pressed.

Computer storage of characters is based on a numerical representation. The details of this vary between applications, and are not important to us here. We shall assume that characters are associated with each integer from 32 to 126 as shown in Table 4.1. These particular allocations are in common use, and are referred to as ASCII codes. We shall write **C** for the set of characters given in Table 4.1.

ASCII can be pronounced "askey". It stands for "American Standard Code for Information Interchange".

The ASCII code 32 corresponds to a "space" in text. It is what you obtain when you press the spacebar in word-processing.

Table 4.1   Characters with ASCII codes between 32 and 126

32		64	@	96	`
33	!	65	A	97	a
34	"	66	B	98	b
35	#	67	C	99	c
36	$	68	D	100	d
37	%	69	E	101	e
38	&	70	F	102	f
39	'	71	G	103	g
40	(	72	H	104	h
41	)	73	I	105	i
42	*	74	J	106	j
43	+	75	K	107	k
44	,	76	L	108	l
45	-	77	M	109	m
46	.	78	N	110	n
47	/	79	O	111	o
48	0	80	P	112	p
49	1	81	Q	113	q
50	2	82	R	114	r
51	3	83	S	115	s
52	4	84	T	116	t
53	5	85	U	117	u
54	6	86	V	118	v
55	7	87	W	119	w
56	8	88	X	120	x
57	9	89	Y	121	y
58	:	90	Z	122	z
59	;	91	[	123	{
60	<	92	\	124	|
61	=	93	]	125	}
62	>	94	∧	126	~
63	?	95	–		

Translation back and forth between a character and its numerical representation is achieved using two functions: *ASC* and *CHR*. The function *CHR* has a natural number as input and outputs the corresponding character, as given in Table 4.1. We shall be concerned only with the characters in the table, so we take *CHR* to have the domain $\{n \in \mathbb{N} : 32 \leq n \leq 126\}$. The function *ASC* has the reverse effect: it inputs a character and outputs the corresponding numerical code.

ASC can be pronounced "ask" as in "askey", and *CHR* as "ker".

Most computer applications associate a character with each integer from 0 to 255, but we are not concerned with the others here.

Activity 4.5   Practice with characters

Let $A = \{n \in \mathbb{N} : 32 \leq n \leq 126\}$.

(a) What is the signature of each of the functions ASC and CHR?

(b) What is each of: (i) $CHR(74)$;   (ii) $ASC(\text{'J'})$;   (iii) $ASC(\text{'j'})$;
(iv) $CHR(106)$?

(c) What is $ASC(CHR(74))$? Can your result be generalised? For $n \in A$, can you say what $ASC(CHR(n))$ must be?

(d) What is $CHR(ASC(\text{'j'}))$? Can you generalise your result?

(e) What can you say about the relationship between the functions ASC and CHR? (Think back to Section 5 of Chapter A4.)

(f) Suppose that a word-processing package has a key combination that changes an upper-case letter to the corresponding lower-case letter, and vice versa. It leaves other characters in **C** unchanged. Call the function that is being evaluated here $CHANGE$. Give the signature of $CHANGE$, and describe its rule algebraically, using ASC and CHR and operations on numbers.

Comment

(a) The signature for ASC is $\mathbf{C} \longrightarrow \mathbf{A}$.
The signature for CHR is $\mathbf{A} \longrightarrow \mathbf{C}$.

(b) In each case, you need to read the value from Table 4.1.

   (i) $CHR(74) = \text{'J'}$

   (ii) $ASC(\text{'J'}) = 74$

   (iii) $ASC(\text{'j'}) = 106$

   (iv) $CHR(106) = \text{'j'}$

(c) $ASC(CHR(74)) = ASC(\text{'J'})$ (evaluate $CHR(74)$ first)
$$= 74$$

Notice that after applying first CHR then ASC to 74, you are back to 74. In general, suppose that you start with any number n in A. Then $CHR(n)$ is the character given to the right of n in Table 4.1. Moreover, $ASC(CHR(n))$ is the numerical ASCII code of the character $CHR(n)$, which you find to the left of $CHR(n)$ in the table. So to find $ASC(CHR(n))$, all you do is find n in the table, look to its right, then look back to the left – and read off n again. So for any $n \in A$, we have

$$ASC(CHR(n)) = n.$$

(d) $CHR(ASC(\text{'j'})) = CHR(106)$
$$= \text{'j'}$$

Again, we are back where we started. And for a general character c, a similar argument to that in (c) explains why we must have

$$CHR(ASC(c)) = c,$$

for any $c \in \mathbf{C}$.

(e) In Section 5 of Chapter A4 you met the idea of an *inverse* function. Remember that a function G is the inverse function of a function F, if G undoes F. Here, ASC undoes CHR and CHR undoes ASC. So ASC is the inverse function of CHR and CHR is the inverse function of ASC.

(f) *CHANGE* inputs a character and outputs a character, so it has
signature $\mathbf{C} \longrightarrow \mathbf{C}$. Looking at Table 4.1 you can see that each
lower-case letter has a numerical code that is exactly 32 larger than
that of the corresponding upper-case letter. So you can describe the
rule for *CHANGE* as:

$$CHANGE(c) = \begin{cases} CHR(ASC(c) - 32) \text{ if } 97 \leq ASC(c) \leq 122; \\ CHR(ASC(c) + 32) \text{ if } 65 \leq ASC(c) \leq 90; \\ c, \text{ otherwise.} \end{cases}$$

The first line changes a lower-case letter to upper-case, the second line
changes an upper-case letter to lower-case and the final line leaves the
other characters unchanged. Figure 4.2 illustrates the steps needed in
the first line to change a lower-case letter to upper-case.

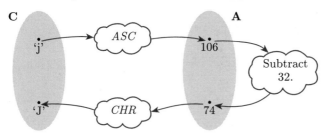

Figure 4.2   Obtaining 'J' from 'j'

The section continues overleaf.

4.5   Operations as functions

To perform calculations on numbers, a computer needs to be able to add or subtract numbers, for example. Can these processes be seen as functions? Certainly, subtracting a constant value, such as 6, from an input number corresponds to a function. We might call it *TAKESIX*, where

$$TAKESIX : \mathbb{R} \longrightarrow \mathbb{R}$$
$$x \longmapsto x - 6.$$

But what about the process of subtraction in general?

Activity 4.6   Thinking about subtraction

If a computer is to subtract, how many inputs does it require? What output does it produce? What signature would you expect a function subtracting real numbers to have?

Comment

Subtraction always involves two numbers (as in $5 - 6$, $4.3 - 1.76$, or whatever). And you can subtract any real number from any other real number, without restriction. So subtraction as a function will have domain $\mathbb{R} \times \mathbb{R}$. Since the result of subtraction is a single number, the function has codomain $\mathbb{R}$. Calling a general function that subtracts real numbers *SUB*, we have $SUB : \mathbb{R} \times \mathbb{R} \longrightarrow \mathbb{R}$, where $SUB(x, y) = x - y$.

You can see addition and multiplication of real numbers as functions in a similar way. Each of these functions has signature $\mathbb{R} \times \mathbb{R} \longrightarrow \mathbb{R}$.

Activity 4.7   Identifying signatures

Give the signature of each of the following functions.

(a) *DIV*, that divides real numbers.

(b) *EQUCHR*, that compares two characters to determine whether or not they are the same.

Many calculators label this button $+/-$.

(c) *CHGSIGN*, corresponding to the "change sign" button on a calculator (that changes 4.1 to -4.1 and -3.27 to 3.27, for example).

Comment

(a) Division requires two real number inputs and produces a real number output. This time, though, the number by which you divide must not be 0. Thus, if the rule of *DIV* is $DIV(x, y) = x/y$, then the domain of the division function is

$$\{(x, y) \in \mathbb{R} \times \mathbb{R} : y \neq 0\}.$$

Calling this set Z, we have $DIV : Z \longrightarrow \mathbb{R}$.

(b) *EQUCHR* will have two characters as input and will output a Boolean value. So its signature is $\mathbf{C} \times \mathbf{C} \longrightarrow \mathbf{B}$.

(c) The change sign button operates on a single real number input, and changes the sign of the number operated on, to produce a real number as output. So this process evaluates a function *CHGSIGN*, with signature $\mathbb{R} \longrightarrow \mathbb{R}$, where $CHGSIGN(x) = -x$.

Each of the processes of addition, subtraction and multiplication of real numbers, seen as a function, has domain $\mathbb{R} \times \mathbb{R}$. Functions with this domain are often referred to as **operations on** $\mathbb{R}$. Each of these operations has its own special symbol $(+, -, \times)$, and when these symbols are used they are written *between* the objects on which they operate, as in

$4 - 5.$

This notation, where the operation symbol is written between the objects to be combined, is called **infix** notation. Infix notation applies only to processes combining exactly two objects, one on each side of the symbol. The notation for functions is not constrained in this way, and can cope with functions with any number of inputs: 1, 2, 3, or whatever.

The function *AND*, introduced in Subsection 4.3, has signature $\mathbf{B} \times \mathbf{B} \longrightarrow \mathbf{B}$. So *AND* combines two Boolean values to produce a Boolean value in a way analogous to the combination of two numbers by an arithmetic operation, such as addition or multiplication. We say that *AND* is an **operation on B**. We can also use an infix notation for *AND*. In this case, rather than introduce a separate infix symbol for *AND*, we shall use the name of the function as the operation symbol in infix notation. So we can, for example, write the expression

$AND(AND(4 \leq x, x \leq 20), NOT(x = 10)),$

from the comment on Activity 4.4(c), in infix notation as

$((4 \leq x) \; AND \; (x \leq 20)) \; AND \; NOT(x = 10).$

The expression for the power of a number, 3^4, for example, is not written with an infix notation. You probably do not think of the process of taking a power as an operation. However, there are similarities. For example, it is treated as an operation by Mathcad. There, you would enter $3^{\wedge}4$, with the symbol $\wedge$ representing "to the power of". Mathcad calculates such powers using a function, say *POWER*, with signature $\mathbb{R} \times \mathbb{R} \longrightarrow \mathbb{R}$, where $POWER(x, y) = x^y$. You will be more familiar with thinking of the process of squaring as a function requiring one input, as in $SQUARE : \mathbb{R} \longrightarrow \mathbb{R}$, where $SQUARE(x) = x^2$. But Mathcad treats squaring just as a particular instance of a general power function. It evaluates $POWER(x, 2)$ rather than $SQUARE(x)$. (Some calculators have buttons for both functions: an x^2 button and an x^y button.) Using *POWER*, Mathcad needs only a single algorithm to evaluate *POWER*, rather than separate algorithms to evaluate each of x^2, x^3, x^4, and so on. (In fact, this later approach could not evaluate all the cases covered by the general *POWER* function, since there are infinitely many different possibilities!) This use of the function *POWER* has some effect on the way Mathcad handles algebraic expressions, as you will see in Sections 6 and 7.

Activity 4.8 More Handbook annotation

This section contains a number of new terms, such as

character, signature and operation.

Have a look at the examples in Figure 4.3 opposite of how draft *Handbook* entries for some of these terms might be annotated. Think about how *you* might annotate one or more of these entries. Add any annotation you think might be helpful, in pencil, to these entries in your *Handbook*, and record your annotation on Learning File Sheet 2.

Comment

Many people find illustrative examples helpful. Choose examples that help to bring an idea to life for you. Make sure your examples are correct! Sometimes you may want to expand on *Handbook* entries, or to give alternative wordings.

Handbook annotation is a personal matter, so it is not possible to describe the examples in Figure 4.3 as "good" or "bad". However, I would think that, with the exception of the first, these are all appropriate styles of annotation. The *Handbook* is not a good place to write questions that you want to get answered. These will be a distraction when you come to use it for reference later.

> Is this like a person's signature?
> Does it identify a particular function?
> ASK TUTOR!

SIGNATURE OF A FUNCTION

A statement of the domain and codomain of a function. For example, the signature of *ADDLAST* is

$$X \times SEQ(X) \to SEQ(x)$$

We write

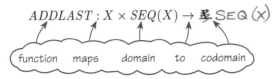

> function maps domain to codomain

OPERATION (ON THE SET X)

A function with signature $X \times X \to X$.

> Egs: $+$; $-$; $\times$ (on R)
> AND (on B)

> An operation is a function which
> acts on two objects from the same set
> to produce an output from that set.
> Eg Addition: R × R → R. This function
> is called an operation on R.

CHARACTER

> (askey)

A symbol obtained by typing the appropriate key on a computer keyboard. (The course only considers printable characters with ASCII codes between 32 and 126.)

> A character is a single symbol
> that appears on the screen.
> Examples are '?', '+' and '3'.
> 'a' and 'A' are different characters.

SET

A collection of objects (without regard to their order, and without repetitions).
See notation entries: $\{x \in X : condition\}$; $\in$; $\notin$; $X \times Y$.

> Examples: DAYS $=$ {Monday, Tuesday, ..., Sunday}
> R – the set of all real numbers
> $\{x \in R: x \neq 2\}$ – the set of all real numbers <u>except 2</u>.
> $\{(x, y) \in R \times R: x \neq 0\}$.

Figure 4.3 Some examples of *Handbook* annotations

Summary of Section 4

Various notations for writing sets have been introduced. A set with just a few members can be described by listing all its members between curly brackets. The notation $\{x \in X : condition\}$ describes the set of all objects from X satisfying the specified condition. The set of pairs (x, y), with x in X and y in Y, is written $X \times Y$. Two sets of "non-number" objects have been introduced: $\mathbf{B} = \{\text{true}, \text{false}\}$, the set of Boolean values, and $\mathbf{C}$, the set of characters.

These notations were used in describing the domains and codomains of various functions. You met the functions AND and NOT, which can be used in describing conditions algebraically. You also saw how operations, such as addition and multiplication, and comparisons, such as $>$, can be regarded as functions.

The word "signature" was introduced, meaning a statement of the domain and codomain of a function: for example, $\mathbf{B} \times \mathbf{B} \longrightarrow \mathbf{B}$ is the signature of the function AND.

Exercises for Section 4

Exercise 4.1

(a) List the members of the set $G \times H$, where

$$G = \{\text{'a'}, \text{'b'}, \text{'c'}\} \quad \text{and} \quad H = \{1, 2\}.$$

(b) Use curly bracket notation to describe:

(i) the set of natural numbers between 4 and 17, inclusive;

(ii) the set of real numbers which, when cubed, give a result whose magnitude is less than 6 (that is, between -6 and 6).

(c) Let $|x|$ have the meaning mentioned in Exercise 2.1 (that is, for $x \in \mathbb{R}$, $|x|$ is x if $x \geq 0$, and is $-x$ if $x < 0$).

Let $A = \{x \in \mathbb{R} : |x - 3| < 5\}$.

Say whether each of the following is true or false.

✓ (i) $1 \in A$ $|1-3| = |-2| = 2$

✗ (ii) $10 \in A$ $|10-3| = |7| = 7$

✓ (iii) $7.32 \in A$ $|7.32-3| = 4.32$

Exercise 4.2

Express each of the following conditions algebraically, using only functions from the list

$ASC, CHR, AND, NOT, \geq, \leq$ and $=$ for real numbers.

(a) The character c is a lower-case letter.

(b) The real numbers x and y must not both be 0.

5 Sequences

In this section we compare and contrast finite sequences and sets, illustrate some functions which operate on finite sequences, and introduce notation for the sum of a finite sequence of numbers.

5.1 Finite sequences

A sequence is a list of items, written in a specific order. You met examples of sequences in Chapter A1, and saw in Chapter A4 that a sequence can be defined as a function with domain $\mathbb{N}^*$. When a formula such as

$$u_n = \tfrac{1}{2}n(n+1)$$

is used to define a sequence, we look at the values of the formula for $n = 0, 1, 2, 3$, and so on. Thus, for each value $n \in \mathbb{N}^*$, we have an output value u_n. So $n \longmapsto u_n$ is a function with domain $\mathbb{N}^*$. The ordering of the numbers in $\mathbb{N}^*$ gives the order for the terms of the sequence. The formula for u_n above gives the sequence values

> As you have seen in Block A, we may be interested in only $n = 1, 2, 3, \ldots$.

0, 1, 3, 6, 10, and so on,

in that order.

The sequences you met in Block A are *infinite* sequences. There are as many terms in these sequences as there are numbers in $\mathbb{N}^*$, that is, infinitely many! Now a good deal of machine computation is based on the handling of sequences. However, *infinite* sequences are a problem for a computer, since any machine has only a finite amount of storage. For a sequence with a formula, such as $u_n = \frac{1}{2}n(n+1)$, we can use the formula to provide an algorithm to calculate the values of u_n. But even then, the computer will have a maximum size of integer that it can store, and this will impose a limit on the values of n it can handle. For example, Mathcad can handle integers up to only about 10^{307}. That may seem big enough for all practical purposes, but I do not want to get into a discussion of what that might mean here! Certainly, to a mathematician, there is a great difference between the set of numbers

$$A = \{n \in \mathbb{N}^* : 0 \le n \le 10^{307}\}$$

and $\mathbb{N}^*$ itself. The set A may be large, but it is finite, while $\mathbb{N}^*$ is not.

For computers, we need to consider *finite* rather than infinite sequences. A **finite sequence** is a *finite* list of items in a specific order. So, for example,

$$\langle 1, 4, 9, 16, 25 \rangle,$$
$$\langle 1, 0, 1, 0, 1, 0, 1, 0 \rangle,$$
$$\langle 1, 4, 1, 5, 9, 2, 6, 5 \rangle$$

and

$$\langle \text{'t'}, \text{'o'}, \text{'r'}, \text{'t'}, \text{'o'}, \text{'i'}, \text{'s'}, \text{'e'} \rangle$$

are examples of finite sequences. As earlier, we have used angle brackets $\langle \, \rangle$ to show that these are sequences.

The use of different types of brackets enables us to distinguish sequences from sets. Without brackets you could not tell whether

$$1, 4, 9, 16, 25$$

is intended to be a set or a sequence. To show that a set is intended, we would enclose these numbers in curly brackets { }; if a sequence were intended, then angle brackets $\langle\,\rangle$ would be used.

The ideas "set" and "sequence" have some similarity. Each is a collection of items. However, they are different. The key distinctions are *ordering* and *repetition*. The items in a sequence appear in a particular order. The items in a set are not ordered. To write down a particular set, we may have to give its elements in some order, but this order is not important. The *sets*

Although the commonest couplings are "element of a set" and "term of a sequence", you will meet the words member, element, term, item and object, as suits the context.

$$A = \{1, 4, 9, 16, 25\}$$

and

$$B = \{4, 9, 1, 25, 16\}$$

are the same. In symbols, we write

$$\{1, 4, 9, 16, 25\} = \{4, 9, 1, 25, 16\}$$

or

$$A = B.$$

The *sequences*

$$\langle 1, 4, 9, 16, 25 \rangle$$

and

$$\langle 4, 9, 1, 25, 16 \rangle$$

are *not* the same.

Sets do not contain repetitions of a particular member, while sequences may do so. For example, consider the set *DAYS* giving the days of the week. These days are Monday, Tuesday, etc, and it would be meaningless to include Monday twice in this context. On the other hand, we could use a sequence to list the days on which 1 January fell in the years 1970–79. This sequence is

$\langle$Thursday, Friday, Saturday, Monday, Tuesday, Wednesday, Thursday, Saturday, Sunday, Monday$\rangle$,

and you can see that this does contain repeats.

For a sequence given by a formula, we can extend the angle bracket notation in a way similar to the curly bracket notation. For example,

It is implicit in this notation that n takes values in $\mathbb{N}^*$.

$$\langle 1/n : 1 \leq n \leq 5 \rangle$$

is the sequence

$$\langle 1, 1/2, 1/3, 1/4, 1/5 \rangle.$$

Activity 5.1   Sets and sequences

(a) What is the set of elements appearing in the sequence

$\langle 1, 0, 1, 0, 1, 0, 1, 4, 4, 1 \rangle$? $\{1, 0, 4\}$

(b) Let A be the set of letters in the word 'plate', B be the set of letters in the word 'tappet' and C be the set of letters in the word 'palate'. Which, if any, of the sets A, B and C are the same?

$A = \{p, l, a, te\}$
$B = \{t, a, p, p, e, t\}$ $A = C$
$C = \{p, a, la, ta\}$

(c) List the elements of the sequence

$\langle n + 1/n : 1 \leq n \leq 3 \rangle$. $\{2, 2\frac{1}{2}, 3\frac{1}{3}\}$

(d) Consider the sequence of values produced by starting at 2, and adding to this in steps of 0.2 until you reach 4. Write down the sequence using the $\langle : \rangle$ notation, including an algebraic expression for the elements.

see answer n ∈ N

Comment

Solutions are given on page 76.

5.2 Functions on sequences

In Subsections 3.2 and 3.3 you saw some examples where a computer might handle sequences of characters and of numbers. You needed to be able to add, or delete, an element at the end of a sequence, for example. More generally, these processes are applicable to sequences containing elements of any sort. In expressing such processes as functions, we shall do so for any type of sequence. To express the signature of such functions, we shall use the following notation. We write

$SEQ(X)$

for the set of all *finite* sequences whose elements come from a non-empty set X which may be *any* set. We include in $SEQ(X)$ a special sequence called the **empty sequence**. This is a sequence with no elements, and we write it $\langle \rangle$. For example, in Subsection 3.2 you needed to deal with a situation where the memory contained "no text". There, you were dealing with sequences of characters (from $SEQ(\mathbf{C})$), and "no text" would be represented by the empty sequence. For example:

$\langle$ 'a', 'b', 'c' $\rangle \in SEQ(\mathbf{C})$;

$\langle 5, 17, 4, 8 \rangle \in SEQ(\mathbb{N})$;

$\langle$ true, false, true, false, true $\rangle \in SEQ(\mathbf{B})$;

$\langle \rangle \in SEQ(X)$,   for any set X.

As an example of a function on sequences, consider the process of deleting the last element of a sequence. This will, for example, turn $\langle 1, 2, 3 \rangle$ into $\langle 1, 2 \rangle$, and $\langle 5, 2 \rangle$ into $\langle 5 \rangle$. It will turn $\langle 5 \rangle$ into the empty sequence $\langle \rangle$. Since $\langle \rangle$ has no elements, it is not appropriate to think of the process of deleting its last element. So the empty sequence $\langle \rangle$ is not in the domain of the function.

Let $DELLAST$ be the function that deletes the last element of a sequence ($DELLAST$ was introduced in Section 3). Then the domain of $DELLAST$ is the set of non-empty finite sequences. I shall write $NESEQ(X)$ for the set of all non-empty finite sequences with members from X. So

$NESEQ(X) = \{s \in SEQ(X) : s \neq \langle \rangle\}$.

The function $DELLAST$ has codomain $SEQ(X)$, so its signature is $NESEQ(X) \longrightarrow SEQ(X)$.

As in Section 3, we shall use the same name for the function $DELLAST$ whatever the set X may be. This corresponds to the situation one would expect in a computer programming language, where processes would be available to handle sequences in general, irrespective of the type of object in the sequences.

Activity 5.2   LAST and ADDLAST

(a) Give the signature of each of the following functions, which were also introduced in Section 3. (In each case, the elements of the sequence come from X, which may be any set.)

   (i) The function $LAST$, that gives the last element in a sequence.

   (ii) The function $ADDLAST$, that adds a given element from X to the end of a sequence.

(b) What is each of the following?

   (i) $ADDLAST(\text{'a'}, \langle \rangle)$

   (ii) $LAST(\langle 0 \rangle)$

   (iii) $LAST(\langle \rangle)$

Comment

Solutions are given on page 76.

For example, this might be the condition in a repeat ... until structure. The instructions are repeated until the condition is true

In Section 3 you met algorithms that include conditions such as

   seq contains no elements,

where *seq* is a sequence. To determine the outcome, true or false, of such a condition, a computer would need to have a suitable function available.

Activity 5.3   Is the sequence empty?

The function $ISEMPTY$ determines whether or not a sequence is empty.

(a) Describe a function that could serve this purpose. Suggest a signature and rule for $ISEMPTY$.

(b) Using $ISEMPTY$, express algebraically the condition

   seq contains no elements,

where *seq* is a sequence.

Comment

(a) We can use a function that inputs a sequence, and gives the output true or false, depending on whether or not the sequence s is empty. This function has domain $SEQ(X)$ and codomain $\mathbf{B}$. So

$$ISEMPTY : SEQ(X) \longrightarrow \mathbf{B},$$

where $ISEMPTY(\langle \rangle) = \text{true}$, and $ISEMPTY(s) = \text{false}$ if $s \neq \langle \rangle$.

(b) This condition can be expressed as

$$ISEMPTY(seq).$$

You may have written

$$ISEMPTY(seq) = \text{true}.$$

The "= true" is not needed, since the expression $ISEMPTY(seq)$ gives a Boolean value true or false, and so already is of the form required for a condition.

Activity 5.4   An algorithm using sequence functions

In the following algorithm, s is a sequence.

> If s is empty, then the calculated value is 0. Otherwise proceed as below.
>
> Set *memone* equal to 0.   (1)
> Set *memtwo* equal to s.   (2)
> Repeat the instructions:
> >   add 1 to the value in *memone*;   (3)
> >   delete the last element from the sequence in *memtwo*;   (4)
>
> until the sequence in *memtwo* is empty.
> The calculated value is in *memone*.

(a) Trace the values stored in *memone* and *memtwo* when $s = \langle 2, 3, 6, 6 \rangle$ is input to this algorithm. Show which line is used at each step.

(b) Describe the function evaluated by this algorithm. Give its signature, and express its rule in words.

(c) Assume that the functions *DELLAST* and *ISEMPTY*, as described above, are available, as well as operations on numbers. Express the algorithm algebraically.

Comment

(a) A trace is given below.

Line	*memone*	*memtwo*
1	0	—
2	0	$\langle 2, 3, 6, 6 \rangle$
3	1	$\langle 2, 3, 6, 6 \rangle$
4	1	$\langle 2, 3, 6 \rangle$
3	2	$\langle 2, 3, 6 \rangle$
4	2	$\langle 2, 3 \rangle$
3	3	$\langle 2, 3 \rangle$
4	3	$\langle 2 \rangle$
3	4	$\langle 2 \rangle$
4	4	$\langle \rangle$

Since the sequence stored in *memtwo* is now empty, the repetition stops. The final value in *memone* is 4, and this is the value calculated.

(b) The effect of the repetition in the algorithm is to add 1 to *memone* for each element in the input sequence s. So the algorithm counts the number of items in s. If s is empty, then (from the first line) the output of the algorithm is 0. I shall call the function evaluated by this algorithm *LEN*. Thus *LEN* inputs a sequence, and outputs a natural number or zero. So *LEN* has signature $SEQ(X) \longrightarrow \mathbb{N}^*$, and $LEN(s)$ is the number of items in the sequence s (and, in particular, $LEN(\langle \rangle) = 0$).

(c) The algorithm can be expressed algebraically as follows.

> If $ISEMPTY(s)$, then the calculated value is 0. Otherwise proceed as below.
>
> $memone := 0$
> $memtwo := s$
> Repeat the instructions:
> > $memone := memone + 1$
> > $memtwo := DELLAST(memtwo)$
>
> until $ISEMPTY(memtwo)$.
> The calculated value is in *memone*.

Memorising and the Handbook

You may wonder when it is worth while trying to memorise material from the course, be it a result, a technique, or a piece of terminology. A simple answer to that question is *never*. Everything is recorded in the *Handbook*. And if there is something you cannot find in the *Handbook* that you feel you need, you can add it as an annotation. (Add the annotation in a place that is consistent with the structure of the *Handbook*, so that you can find it!)

However, "never" is perhaps too simple an answer. You certainly do not want to be checking in the *Handbook* for the meaning of every piece of terminology you come to when reading the course texts. You need to be able to read text containing technical words that appear regularly without making such references. Examples of such words that appear regularly in this chapter include set, sequence and algorithm. This does *not*, though, mean that you need to memorise some definition of such terms. It means that you need enough feeling for their sense to cope with text that uses them.

When reading ordinary English text, I do not usually stop to check the meaning of unfamiliar words. So long as I feel that I understand the meaning of the text as a whole, I am happy to continue. The same principle can be applied to much of the text in the course material. However, to follow detailed mathematical manipulation, a more exact understanding of notations, particular functions and mathematical processes is needed. In this chapter you have met some notations that are in common use in mathematics, such as the set notation

$$\{x \in X : condition \ on \ x\}.$$

And you have met others that are local to the material discussed in this chapter, such as the particular functions $DELLAST$, $LAST$ and $ADDLAST$. For an item of such "local" terminology, I hope that you will be able to remember its meaning while you are reading this chapter. But there is no point in memorising it. If you need it later, use the *Handbook*.

Where a notation is used frequently, it is useful to remember it. But I hope that you will find such notation is remembered through use, rather than through conscious effort. Occasionally, you may feel that you are looking up some term too often. In that situation, it may be worth while either trying to memorise it, or to have it on a piece of paper in front of you.

Of course, everyone is different! With the question of memorising, you need to find what suits *you*. Some people find it easy to commit things to memory, others find it difficult. But do not mistake rote memory for understanding. Understanding of a concept requires the building up of a complex internalisation of images, analogies and relationships. This is developed through experience and use: working through examples and then practising similar exercises.

The following activity invites you to consider annotation again and may help you assess its value to you.

Activity 5.5 Handbook annotation revisited

Activity 5.4 again used the terminology "the function evaluated by an algorithm". Think again about how you might explain this to a fellow student. Write your explanation on Learning File Sheet 3. Then look again at the definition of this term in the *Handbook*, and at any annotation you made in Activity 3.9. Would you want to change your explanation in any way in the light of this? Would you want to change your annotation in any way?

Look at any annotations you made in response to Activity 4.8. Again, would you want to change your annotations in any way? Can you see any general points about how annotation is useful to you? Use Learning File Sheet 3 to record your ideas on these points.

5.3 Adding sequences of numbers

The functions considered in Subsection 5.2 are applicable to sequences of elements of any sort. Some functions apply only to sequences of numbers. For example, you might want to add the numbers in a sequence. A standard mathematical notation for the sum of a sequence of numbers uses the Greek letter Σ. For a finite sequence $\langle u_n : 1 \leq n \leq k \rangle = \langle u_1, u_2, \ldots, u_k \rangle$, where the values u_n are numbers,

Σ is a (capital) sigma.

$$\sum_{n=1}^{k} u_n$$

means

$$u_1 + u_2 + \cdots + u_k.$$

$\displaystyle\sum_{n=1}^{k} u_n$ may be read as

"the sum of u_n for $n = 1$ to k".

Where a sequence is given by a formula, such as $u_n = n^2$, this sigma notation may be applied directly to the formula. In the expression

$$\sum_{n=1}^{9} n^2,$$

for example, the $n = 1$ and the 9 give the first and last values of n to be included in the sum. That is, the sequence whose values are being added here is

$$\langle 1^2, 2^2, 3^2, \ldots, 9^2 \rangle \quad \text{or} \quad \langle n^2 : 1 \leq n \leq 9 \rangle.$$

If s is a finite sequence of numbers, the sum of the numbers is denoted by $\sum s$. So if $s = \langle 1, 2, 3, 4 \rangle$,

$$\sum s = 1 + 2 + 3 + 4 = 10.$$

Activity 5.6   Summing a finite sequence of numbers

(a) What is $\sum s$ for each following sequence s?

(i) $\langle 1, 5, 7, 4, 6, 5 \rangle$

(ii) $\langle n^2 : 1 \leq n \leq 4 \rangle$ $1 + 4 + 9 + 16 = 30$

(b) List the terms of the following sequence which is to be summed. Give the numerical value of the sum.

$$\sum_{m=1}^{4} (1 + 0.1m)$$ $\Rightarrow u_m = 1 + 0 \cdot 1m$ $\langle 1 + 0.1m : 1 \leq n \leq 4 \rangle = \langle 1 \cdot 1, 1 \cdot 2, 1 \cdot 3, 1 \cdot 4 \rangle$

$\sum = 5 \cdot 0$

(c) What sequence is being summed in

$$\sum_{n=1}^{120} n^3?$$ $\langle n^3 : 1 \leq n \leq 120 \rangle$

(d) Let *SUM* be a function that sums any non-empty finite sequence of real numbers. What is the signature of the function *SUM*?

$SUM : NESEQ(X) \rightarrow X$
$\text{where } X \in \mathbb{R}$

Comment

Solutions are given on page 76.

Summary of Section 5

A set is a collection of objects whose order is irrelevant, while a sequence lists its objects in a particular order. Computers are able to store only finite sequences, and we use $SEQ(X)$ to denote the set consisting of the empty sequence $\langle \rangle$ and all finite sequences whose members come from the non-empty set X. Various functions handling sequences were discussed. The sigma notation for the sum of the elements in a finite sequence of numbers was introduced.

Exercise for Section 5

Exercise 5.1

Let s be a non-empty finite sequence of numbers.

(a) Give an algorithm to evaluate $\sum s$. Express your algorithm algebraically, using the functions *LAST* and *DELLAST*, and operations on numbers.

(b) Trace your algorithm when $s = \langle 2, 3, 5 \rangle$ is input, and verify that the algorithm produces the correct output.

(*Hint*: You may find it helpful to look at the algorithm in Activity 5.4, and think how you can modify that.)

6 Expressions and trees

In Subsection 1.2 you saw an algorithm showing how the expression

$$(y/4)\exp(y/4 - 2)$$

can be evaluated in a series of steps. Each step consisted of evaluating a single operation or function: subtracting two numbers, or finding an exponential, for example. In this section you will meet a diagrammatic representation of an expression, showing how it is made up of such "elementary" steps. This representation is called a *tree*. You will see how to construct and interpret such trees. The representation of an expression as a tree relates to the way Mathcad stores expressions. You will investigate this in Section 7.

The value of the expression $(3 + 4) \times 9$ is found by multiplying the numbers $3 + 4$ and 9. And $3 + 4$ is found by adding 3 and 4. Figure 6.1 shows this as a function box picture.

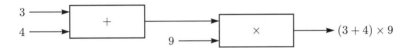

Figure 6.1

In Figure 6 this function box picture has been turned on its side, and the boxes have been removed. This results in a form of diagram called a **tree**. Any valid expression has a corresponding tree diagram, which shows the way the expression is put together from its component elements. Figure 6 shows the tree for the expression $(3 + 4) \times 9$.

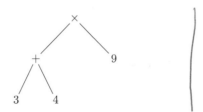

Figure 6.2   Tree diagram for the expression $(3 + 4) \times 9$

Conventionally, such tree diagrams are pictured growing downwards, so that the $\times$ at the top is called the **root** of the tree. The construction, interpretation and use of tree diagrams is discussed in the audio band *Expression trees*.

Now listen to Audio Tape 2, Band 1, 'Expression trees'.

Frame 1

An example

Expression $(3 + 4) \times 9$

Tree

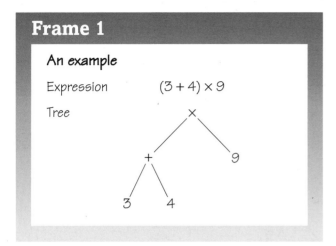

Frame 2

Forming a tree

Expression $(3 + 4) \times 9$

Step 1

Step 2

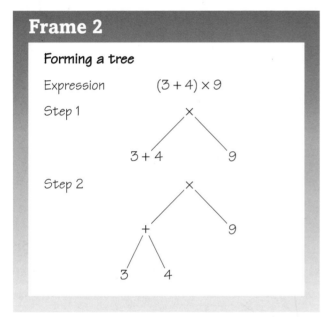

Frame 3

Naming the parts

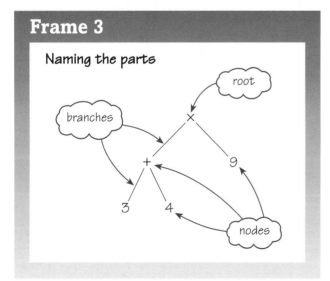

Frame 4

What goes where

Expression $5 \times (\exp(9 - 2))$

Tree

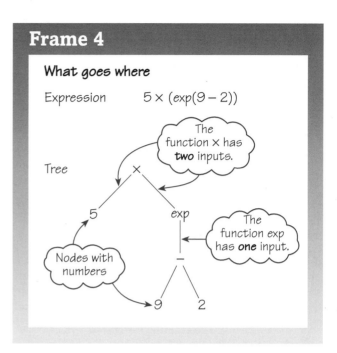

Frame 5

Read from left to right

Expression $9 - 2$

Tree 1

Expression $2 - 9$

Tree 2

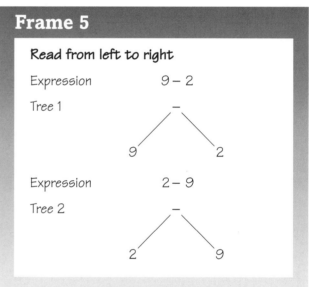

Frame 6

Activity 6.1

Give expression trees for:

Expression 1 $(6 \times 7) + \sin(3 - 1)$

Expression 2 $\exp((y/4) - 2)$

Expression 3 $(y/4) \times \exp((y/4) - 2)$

Comments are in:

Frame 19

Frame 20

Frame 21.

Frame 7

Invalid expressions

Example 1 $5 \times 4 +$

Example 2 $(3 + 4 \times 7/8$

Attempt at
tree for
Example 1

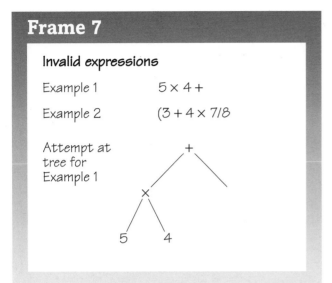

Frame 8

From tree to expression

Tree

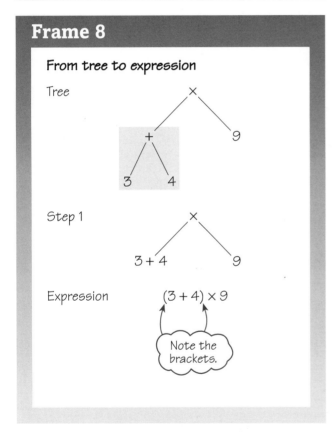

Step 1

Expression $(3 + 4) \times 9$

Note the
brackets.

Frame 9

You do it

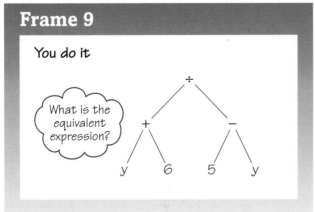

What is the
equivalent
expression?

Frame 10

The answer

Step 1

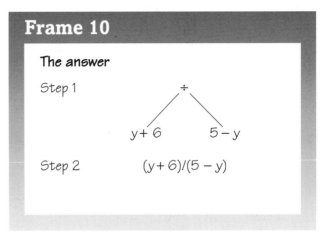

Step 2 $(y + 6)/(5 - y)$

Frame 11

Filling in details

Expression 4 $5x - 6$

Expression 5 $(5 \times x) - 6$

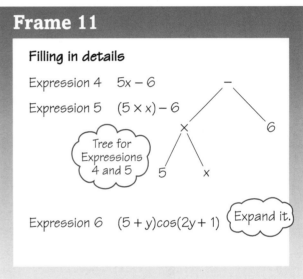

Tree for
Expressions
4 and 5

Expression 6 $(5 + y)\cos(2y + 1)$ Expand it.

Frame 12

A more complicated example

Expression 6 $(5 + y)\cos(2y + 1)$

Expression 6
"expanded" $(5 + y) \times (\cos((2 \times y) + 1))$

Tree

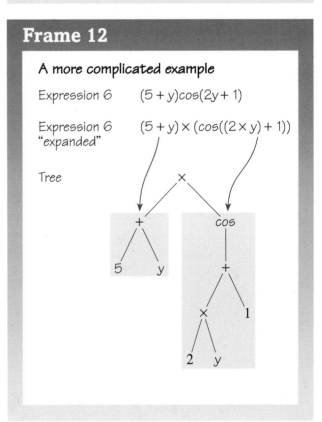

61

Frame 13

Calculating Expression 6

Instruction		Value in:	memone	memtwo
(1)	memone := y		y	–
(2)	memone := 2 × memone		$2 \times y$	–
(3)	memone := memone + 1		$2y + 1$	–
(4)	memone := cos(memone)		$\cos(2y+1)$	–
(5)	memtwo := y		$\cos(2y+1)$	y
(6)	memtwo := 5 + memtwo		$\cos(2y+1)$	$5+y$
(7)	memone := memtwo × memone		$(5+y)\cos(2y+1)$	$5+y$

The calculated value is in *memone.*

Frame 14

A power

Expression x^5

Tree

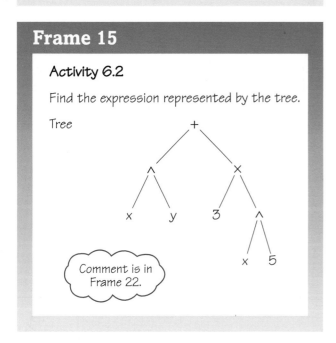

Frame 15

Activity 6.2

Find the expression represented by the tree.

Tree

Comment is in Frame 22.

Frame 16

One expression ... two interpretations ...

Expression $5x/(x^2 + 1)$

Interpretation 1 $(5 \times x)/(x^2 + 1)$

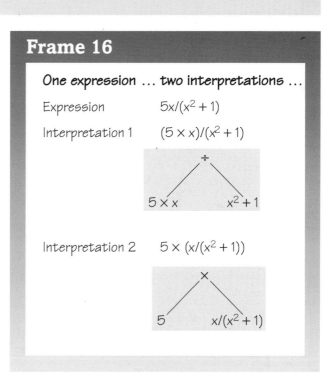

Interpretation 2 $5 \times (x/(x^2 + 1))$

Frame 17

... two trees

Interpretation 1 $(5 \times x)/(x^2 + 1)$

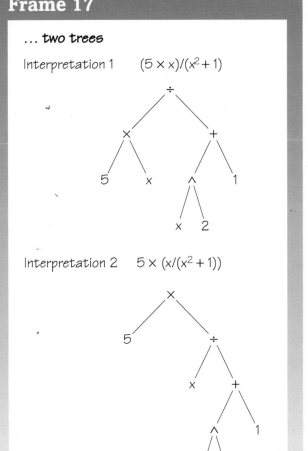

Interpretation 2 $5 \times (x/(x^2 + 1))$

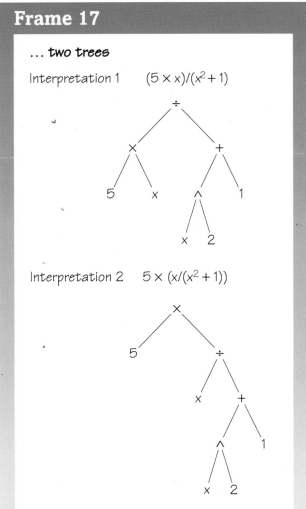

Frame 18

Three inputs

Expression	Meaning
$5 \times IF(a > b, a, b) =$	$5a,$ if $a > b,$
	$5b,$ if $a \leq b.$

Tree

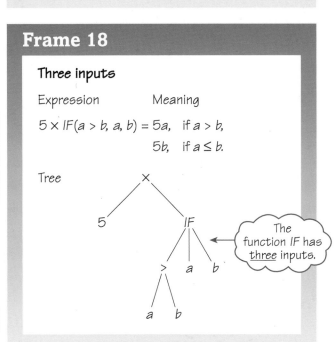

The function *IF* has <u>three</u> inputs.

Frame 19

Expression 1

Expression 1 $(6 \times 7) + \sin(3 - 1)$

Tree

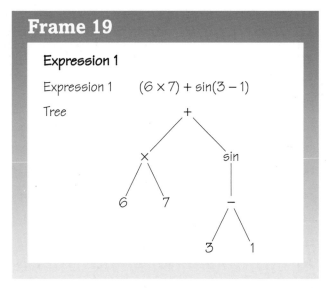

Frame 20

Expression 2

Expression 2 $\exp((y/4) - 2)$

Tree

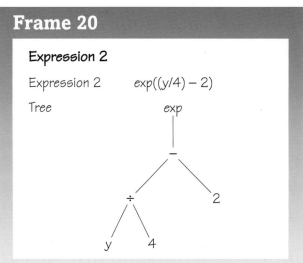

Frame 21

Expression 3

Expression 3 $(y/4) \times \exp((y/4) - 2)$

Tree

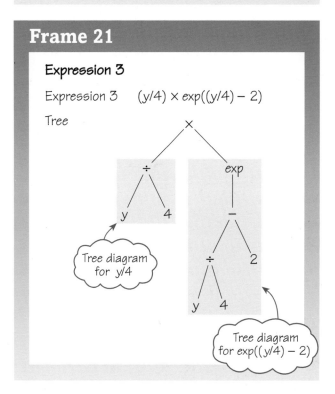

Tree diagram for $y/4$

Tree diagram for $\exp((y/4) - 2)$

Frame 22

Comment on Activity 6.2

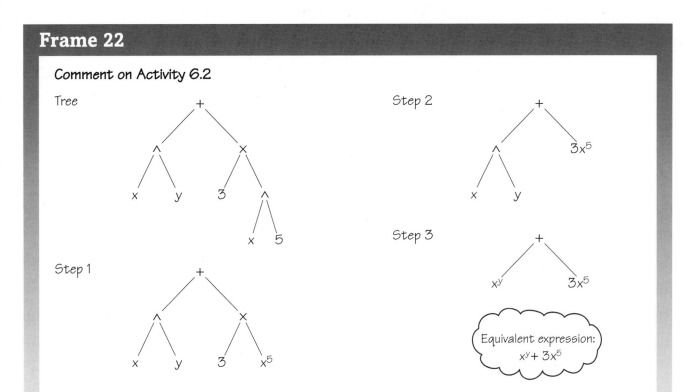

Tree

Step 1

Step 2

Step 3

Equivalent expression:
$x^y + 3x^5$

Activity 6.3   Interpreting trees

Give the expression equivalent to each of the trees in Figure 6.3.

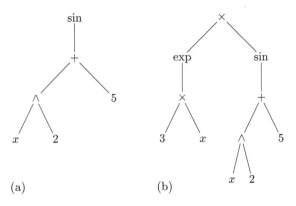

Figure 6.3

Comment

Solutions are given on page 76.

Activity 6.4   Constructing trees

Give the tree diagram for each of the following expressions.

(a) $x/(2 - 3x)$

(b) $x^4 + 3^y$

(c) $5(x + y) + (4x - 3y)$

Comment

You need to identify the implicit multiplications in the expressions, and also to include $\wedge$ to represent "to the power of", where appropriate. With these shown explicitly, the expressions become as given below.

(a) $x/(2 - (3 \times x))$

(b) $(x\wedge 4) + (3\wedge y)$

(c) $(5 \times (x + y)) + ((4 \times x) - (3 \times y))$

The trees are given in Figure 6.4.

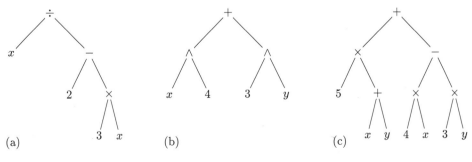

Figure 6.4

Activity 6.5   Trees and algorithms

The following algorithm gives a sequence of evaluation steps (for an input value $x \in \mathbb{R}$).

$memone := x$
$memtwo := 3 \times memone$
$memtwo := memtwo - 2$
$memtwo := \exp(memtwo)$
$memthree := 5 \times memone$
$memthree := \cos(memthree)$
$memthree := memthree \times memtwo$

The calculated value is $memthree$.

(a) Trace the values stored in $memone$, $memtwo$ and $memthree$ as this evaluation is executed. What is the value calculated?

(b) Find the expression represented by the tree given in Figure 6.5. Collapse the tree step by step, and compare the values you obtain at each step with the values in your trace in (a).

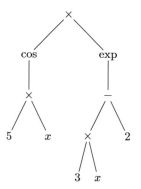

Figure 6.5

Comment

Solutions are given on page 77.

Summary of Section 6

Tree diagrams were introduced as a way of representing the structure of numeric and algebraic expressions. Corresponding to a given tree there is a unique expression, but some expressions may be represented by more than one tree, each one corresponding to a different way of adding brackets to the expression. The steps in collapsing a given tree relate to the sequence of evaluation instructions for the corresponding expression.

7 Editing expressions in Mathcad

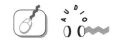

It is tricky to edit expressions in Mathcad until you have some feeling for how it handles expressions. The ideas in Section 6 throw some light on this.

This section is based on work with Mathcad, and so is in Computer Book B. There is also an audio band associated with this section that provides extra discussion of the ideas and further practice. Below there is an extended summary of the section.

Refer to Computer Book B for the work in this section.

Summary of Section 7

In an expression such as

$$\frac{y}{2 - 3y},$$

certain parts of the expression (such as $2 - 3y$) themselves form expressions. We refer to such parts as **subexpressions**. A subexpression has its own tree, and this will appear as part of the tree for the whole expression. It will be a part consisting of a node, together with all of the tree below that node. We refer to such a part of a tree as a **subtree**. These terms are illustrated in Figure 7.1.

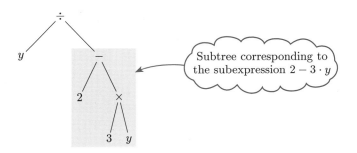

Subtree corresponding to the subexpression $2 - 3 \cdot y$

Figure 7.1 The tree for the subexpression $2 - 3y$ is a subtree of the tree for the expression $y/(2 - 3y)$

Mathcad has two different ways of navigating within an expression: **selection-box** mode and **insertion-point** mode (see Figure 7.2). Selection box mode is based on the tree structure of an expression, while insertion-point mode treats the expression essentially as a sequence of characters.

$$\frac{y}{2 - 3 \cdot y} \qquad \frac{y}{2 - 3y}$$

(a)   (b)

Figure 7.2 Examples of Mathcad displays in (a) selection-box mode and (b) insertion-point mode

In selection-box mode, the position of the box can be changed by use of the arrow keys. To predict the effect of the arrow keys, we look at the tree for the expression. At a given moment, the selection box surrounds a subexpression. The node at the root of the subtree corresponding to the boxed subexpression is referred to as the **current node**. (So, for example, in the situation in Figure 7.3(a), the current node is −.) The effect of each arrow key is to move the current node in a fairly natural way, as given below.

The [↑] key moves the current node up one level in the tree.

The [↓] key moves the current node down one level in the tree, choosing the node below and to the right.

The [←] key moves the current node to the left, staying at the same level in the tree.

The [→] key moves the current node to the right, staying at the same level in the tree.

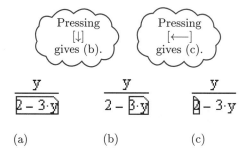

(a)   (b)   (c)

Figure 7.3   Examples of the effect of arrow keys in selection-box mode on the subexpression in Figure 7.1

These effects are not always possible; for example, the current node cannot move up one level if the entire expression is already boxed, so that the current node is at the root of the whole tree. In these circumstances, the arrow keys may have no effect. When the current node is at the "bottom" of the tree, the [↓] key has the effect of moving Mathcad out of selection-box mode and into insertion-point.

In selection-box mode, pressing the [Backspace] key deletes the operator at the current node (which is replaced by a placeholder). If some other operator is then typed, that operator is placed at the current node. So, for example, to change $y/(2 - 3y)$ to $y/(2 + 3y)$, proceed as follows.

Use the arrow keys to get the selection box around $2 - 3y$.
Press [Backspace] (so − is replaced by a placeholder).
Type + (so the placeholder is replace by +).

To correct an error such as a mistyped function name, use insertion-point mode. For example, to correct the incorrect typing of sin in

son$(x^2 + 5)$,

first get Mathcad into insertion-point mode (for example, by repeatedly pressing the [↓] key). Then use the [←] and/or [→] keys to get the insertion point just after the incorrect o in son. Press [Backspace] to erase the o, then type an i.

Navigation in selection-box mode in Mathcad is usually as described above. However, there are a couple of quirks in the way Mathcad structures expressions that lead to slightly unexpected effects when navigating.

It sometimes treats brackets as if they were a separate operation, and gives them a separate node in the tree.

It uses trees with no more than two branches below a node, so its treatment of functions with more than two inputs (such as the function if) is a little surprising.

Do not worry about these quirks; guidance will be provided if you are likely to run into them.

8 Rules of manipulation

Earlier in this chapter we considered the structure and interpretation of expressions. We also touched on their evaluation. We have not considered the *manipulation* of expressions. You may do this by hand, or with the help of the Mathcad symbolic processor.

In such manipulation you will have worked with expressions involving numbers, symbols representing numbers, and functions and operations on numbers. Such a manipulation might go like this:

$$y(y + 3) - 3(y + 1)$$
$$= y^2 + 3y - 3y - 3$$
$$= y^2 - 3.$$

How do we know that this is correct? For example, I have replaced

$$y \times (y + 3) \quad \text{by} \quad y \times y + y \times 3.$$

This step may not be obvious in that form in the manipulation because it is incorporated with two other steps. In these steps $y \times y$ is reinterpreted as y^2, and $y \times 3$ is replaced by $3 \times y$ which is then replaced by $3y$.

Each such step is based on some property of real numbers. For example,

$$6 \times (5 + 4) \quad \text{and} \quad 6 \times 5 + 6 \times 4$$

are the same; as are

$$2.2 \times (4.8 + 2.9) \quad \text{and} \quad 2.2 \times 4.8 + 2.2 \times 2.9.$$

(If you do not believe this property, you can work out the values for each example.) Each of these is an instance of the general rule

$$a \times (b + c) = a \times b + a \times c,$$

whatever real numbers a, b and c may represent.

Numbers obey several such rules, and these rules are used in algebraic manipulation. In enabling Mathcad to perform algebra, each such rule will need to have been made explicit, and programmed into the software it uses for processing expressions.

You may well be conscious that you use the rule given above for expanding brackets. But what about the rule that says that it does not matter in which order two numbers are added? For example,

$$6 + 7 = 7 + 6,$$

and

$$1.26 + 6.932 = 6.932 + 1.26.$$

This rule, expressed in a general way, is

$$a + b = b + a,$$

for any numbers a and b in $\mathbb{R}$. Oddly, it is particularly important to be aware that numbers do have such properties – and that you use them in algebra – as you start to study objects *other* than numbers. This is particularly true since there is a tendency among mathematicians to use the same notation ($+$, $\times$), and even the same words (addition, multiplication), for operations on objects other than numbers.

For example, consider a function *JOIN* on sequences defined as follows. For s and t in $SEQ(X)$, $JOIN(s,t)$ is the sequence formed by writing first the sequence s, then the sequence t. For example,

$$JOIN((\text{`a', `n', `t'}), (\text{`h', `i', `l', `l'})) = (\text{`a', `n', `t', `h', `i', `l', `l'}),$$

and

$$JOIN((\,), (\text{`a', `b'})) = (\text{`a', `b'}).$$

The function *JOIN* has signature $SEQ(X) \times SEQ(X) \longrightarrow SEQ(X)$, and so is an *operation* on sequences. (Remember, $+$, $-$ and $\times$ are operations on real numbers.) As with number operations, we can use an infix notation for *JOIN*. This process "puts two sequences together", and some texts write $s + t$ instead of $JOIN(s,t)$. Now just because the symbol $+$ has been used, do not assume that it has all the properties of $+$ on numbers. This is another case where a commonly used notation is potentially confusing. One really should write, for example,

$+_{\mathbb{R}}$,   for addition on $\mathbb{R}$,

and

$+_S$,   for the *JOIN* operation on sequences,

to show that they are *different* processes. But it is rare for such care to be taken, since it can lead to very unwieldy expressions, and the context usually shows which meaning is intended.

Activity 8.1   *Reflecting on properties of number operations* ...

Suggest other properties of real numbers that are used in algebraic manipulation.

Comment

There are various properties that you might have thought of. For example, it does not matter which order two numbers are in when you multiply them. This can be expressed in general as

$a \times b = b \times a,$

where a and b are real numbers.

Another property is

$(a + b) + c = a + (b + c),$

where a, b and c are real numbers. This means that we do not need to include brackets when adding a series of numbers. For example, $(3 + 4) + 5$ and $3 + (4 + 5)$ are the same, and so either can be written as $3 + 4 + 5$ without ambiguity.

Activity 8.2   ... *and on JOIN on sequences*

Does $+_S$ (*JOIN* on sequences) have the property that $u +_S v = v +_S u$, where u and v are any sequences? Can you suggest a different property that $+_{\mathbb{R}}$ and $+_S$ have in common?

71

Comment

No, $+_S$ does not have this property. For example,

$$\langle\text{'a'},\text{'n'},\text{'t'}\rangle +_S \langle\text{'h'},\text{'i'},\text{'l'},\text{'l'}\rangle = \langle\text{'a'},\text{'n'},\text{'t'},\text{'h'},\text{'i'},\text{'l'},\text{'l'}\rangle,$$

but

$$\langle\text{'h'},\text{'i'},\text{'l'},\text{'l'}\rangle +_S \langle\text{'a'},\text{'n'},\text{'t'}\rangle = \langle\text{'h'},\text{'i'},\text{'l'},\text{'l'},\text{'a'},\text{'n'},\text{'t'}\rangle,$$

which is a different sequence.

The property $(a + b) + c = a + (b + c)$ of $+_{\mathbb{R}}$, mentioned in the previous comment, is shared by $+_S$. If u, v and w are sequences, then each of $(u +_S v) +_S w$ and $u +_S (v +_S w)$ is just the sequence formed by writing first the sequence u, then the sequence v and then the sequence w.

For example, if $u = \langle\text{'m'},\text{'a'},\text{'d'}\rangle$, $v = \langle\text{'r'},\text{'i'},\text{'g'}\rangle$ and $w = \langle\text{'a'},\text{'l'}\rangle$, then

$$\begin{aligned} u +_S (v +_S w) &= \langle\text{'m'},\text{'a'},\text{'d'}\rangle +_S \langle\text{'r'},\text{'i'},\text{'g'},\text{'a'},\text{'l'}\rangle \\ &= \langle\text{'m'},\text{'a'},\text{'d'},\text{'r'},\text{'i'},\text{'g'},\text{'a'},\text{'l'}\rangle \end{aligned}$$

and

$$\begin{aligned} (u +_S v) +_S w &= \langle\text{'m'},\text{'a'},\text{'d'},\text{'r'},\text{'i'},\text{'g'}\rangle +_S \langle\text{'a'},\text{'l'}\rangle \\ &= \langle\text{'m'},\text{'a'},\text{'d'},\text{'r'},\text{'i'},\text{'g'},\text{'a'},\text{'l'}\rangle, \end{aligned}$$

which is the same sequence.

Whatever the sequences u, v and w, we obtain the same result in each case, and so

$$(u +_S v) +_S w = u +_S (v +_S w),$$

for any sequences u, v and w.

Summary of Section 8

You have looked briefly at some properties of numbers used in algebraic manipulation. These properties of numbers may – or may not – be shared by operations on objects of other types.

Summary of Chapter B1

The individual section summaries provide a summary of the chapter, and the learning outcomes (below) provide a framework against which you can assess your progress.

Some people move very quickly from finishing one chapter to starting the next. But remember that learning is not just a matter of assembling facts and techniques. You need also to think about *what* you have learned, *how* you have learned it, and how you can use what you have learned in order to move forward. Evaluating your own learning should help you to become more effective in your study.

Learning outcomes

You have been working towards the following learning outcomes.

Terms to know and use

Precedence rule, algorithm, trace, assignment symbol, function evaluated by an algorithm, condition, domain of an expression, character, set, Boolean value, signature of a function, operation on a set, infix notation, finite sequence, tree, root of a tree, node of a tree, branch of a tree, subexpression, subtree.

Symbols and notation to know and use

$\sin^2 x$, $:=$, $\in$, $\notin$, $\{x \in X : condition\ on\ x\}$, $X \times Y$, $\mathbf{B}$, $\mathbf{C}$, $\langle a, b, \ldots, m \rangle$, $\langle f(n) : condition\ on\ n \rangle$, $SEQ(X)$, $\langle \rangle$, $NESEQ(X)$, $\sum_{n=1}^{k} f(n)$, $\sum s$.

Conventions to know and use

Know those conventions commonly used in writing and manipulating mathematical expressions (for example, precedence rules and implicit multiplication).

Use memory labels as values in algorithms.

Mathematical skills

◇ Use sufficient brackets to ensure that an expression is unambiguous.

◇ Express simple algorithms in words.

◇ Express simple algorithms algebraically using assignment, memory locations, standard mathematical functions and other functions introduced in the chapter (*LAST, DELLAST, ADDLAST, ISEMPTY, ASC* and *CHR*).

◇ Trace an algorithm and, where the algorithm is expressed for a general input, find the function it evaluates (giving both the rule and signature of the function).

◇ Determine the effect of the functions *LAST, DELLAST,* and *ADDLAST* on particular sequences.

◇ Determine the effect of the functions *ASC* and *CHR* on particular inputs.

◇ Express conditions algebraically, using the functions *AND* and *NOT*, and conditions such as $=$ and $>$.

◇ Use the function *ISEMPTY* in expressing conditions.

◇ Give the signature of functions, including those corresponding to operations and comparisons (or conditions).

◇ Given a suitable algebraic expression, give an equivalent tree.

◇ Given a tree, give the equivalent algebraic expression.

Mathcad skills

◇ Be aware of the inputs required by, and the effects of, the Mathcad functions angle and if.

◇ Design key sequences to enter expressions into Mathcad, taking account of precedence rules used (or not used) by Mathcad, and its requirement for all multiplications to be explicit.

◇ Enter $=$ as a condition in Mathcad (using the icon $x = y$), and be aware that this is different from both the assignment of a value ($:=$) and from "evaluate" ($=$).

◇ Be aware of the Mathcad error messages "singularity" and "domain error".

◇ Relate the effect of the arrow keys in Mathcad, when navigating within a suitable expression, to the tree structure of that expression.

◇ Correct minor errors in Mathcad expressions.

Learning skills

◇ Manage new terminology, in particular by annotating your *Handbook* in a useful way.

Solutions to Activities

Solution 1.1

This expression is *not* valid. It has three open brackets, (, and two close brackets,). Since these counts are not equal, the expression must be invalid.

Solution 3.2

(a) (i) "bees"

    (ii) 'i'

(b) The effect is to find the piece of text formed by deleting the last character from the text currently stored in memory, and to show this on the screen (replacing the text previously shown on the screen).

(c) The rule for forming the output of $LAST$ is "take the last character of the input text". This does not make sense if the input is the empty text " ", since that does not have a "last character". So the domain of $LAST$ is all non-empty pieces of text. The codomain is all characters used in forming each piece of text.

Solution 3.4

The last character on the screen is $LAST(screen)$. To express that this character is 'u', we can write

$$LAST(screen) = \text{'u'}.$$

Solution 3.5

We can express the algorithm as below.

    $memory := \text{" "}$
    Repeat the instructions:
        $memory := ADDLAST(LAST(screen), memory)$
        $screen := DELLAST(screen)$
    until $LAST(screen) = \text{'u'}$.
    $screen := DELLAST(screen)$
    $screen := ADDLAST(\text{'i'}, screen)$
    Repeat the instructions:
        $screen := ADDLAST(LAST(memory), screen)$
        $memory := DELLAST(memory)$
    until $memory = \text{" "}$.

Solution 4.1

(a) X is the set of natural numbers that lie between 4 and 20 (inclusive), but excluding the number 10.

You may have expressed your answer differently.

(b) (i) $22 \in X$ is false, since the condition $22 \leq 20$ is not true.

    (ii) $15 \in X$ is true, since 15 is in $\mathbb{N}$, and the conditions $4 \leq 15$ and $15 \leq 20$ are both true, and 15 is not equal to 10.

    (iii) $7.23 \in X$ is false, since 7.23 is not in $\mathbb{N}$.

(c) $MONTHS = \{$January, February, March, April, May, June, July, August, September, October, November, December$\}$.

You could equally well have written the months in some other order. Also, you may have used convenient abbreviations for the months.

(d) (i) This is the set

$$\{x \in \mathbb{R} : -\pi/2 < x < \pi/2\}.$$

You could equally well have used some other letter in place of x, for example,

$$\{r \in \mathbb{R} : -\pi/2 < r < \pi/2\}.$$

    (ii) The interval $[0, 6]$ is the set

$$\{x \in \mathbb{R} : 0 \leq x \leq 6\}.$$

Again, you could have used any other letter in place of x.

Solution 4.2

(a) Each of the pairs in (i), (ii) and (iii) consists of two real numbers, and so is in $\mathbb{R} \times \mathbb{R}$. However, for the pair in (ii) the condition $x \neq 0$ is false. So (i) and (iii) are in the given set, but (ii) is not.

(b) Each of (i) and (ii) consists of a triple of the form (true/false, real number, real number), and so is in $\mathbf{B} \times \mathbb{R} \times \mathbb{R}$. In (iii) the elements in the triple are in the wrong order, since the first element is in $\mathbb{R}$, not $\mathbf{B}$ (and the second in $\mathbf{B}$, not $\mathbb{R}$). (iv) gives a pair, not a triple. So (i) and (ii) are in $\mathbf{B} \times \mathbb{R} \times \mathbb{R}$, but (iii) and (iv) are not.

(c) The pairs (n, m) come from the set $\mathbb{N} \times MONTHS$. You also need to take account of the numbers of days in each month. These lead to the complicated condition given below. Note that *everything* after the colon constitutes the condition that the pair (n, m) must satisfy.

DATESIN97

$$= \{(n, m) \in \mathbb{N} \times MONTHS :$$

> if m = January, then $1 \leq n \leq 31$;
>
> if m = February, then $1 \leq n \leq 28$;
>
> if m = March, then $1 \leq n \leq 31$;
>
> if m = April, then $1 \leq n \leq 30$;
>
> if m = May, then $1 \leq n \leq 31$;
>
> if m = June, then $1 \leq n \leq 30$;
>
> if m = July, then $1 \leq n \leq 31$;
>
> if m = August, then $1 \leq n \leq 31$;
>
> if m = September, then $1 \leq n \leq 30$;
>
> if m = October, then $1 \leq n \leq 31$;
>
> if m = November, then $1 \leq n \leq 30$;
>
> if m = December, then $1 \leq n \leq 31\}$.

You probably have written these conditions in a different way.

(d) The plane consists of all pairs of real numbers, so it is the set $\mathbb{R} \times \mathbb{R}$. A circle of radius r is the set

$$\{(x, y) \in \mathbb{R} \times \mathbb{R} : x^2 + y^2 = r^2\}.$$

Solution 5.1

(a) This set is $\{1, 0, 4\}$. Or it could just as well be written as $\{0, 1, 4\}$ or $\{1, 4, 0\}$, for example.

(b) The set A is $\{\text{'a', 'e', 'l', 'p', 't'}\}$. The set B is $\{\text{'a', 'e', 'p', 't'}\}$, which is different from A. The set C is the same as A. In symbols: $A = C$; $A \neq B$.

(c) You obtain the elements of the sequence by setting n equal to 1, 2, 3, in turn, in the formula $n + 1/n$. This gives

$$\langle 2, 2\tfrac{1}{2}, 3\tfrac{1}{3} \rangle.$$

(d) This is the sequence

$$\langle 2 + 0.2n : 0 \leq n \leq 10 \rangle.$$

To check that this is correct, remember that this notation represents the sequence obtained by putting n, in turn, equal to each of the integers 0, 1, 2, 3, ..., 10, in the formula $2 + 0.2n$. This gives values starting at 2 (when $n = 0$) and increasing in steps of 0.2 to 4 (when $n = 10$).

This is not the only correct answer. For example, you could equally well have given

$$\langle 1.8 + 0.2n : 1 \leq n \leq 11 \rangle,$$

which gives exactly the same sequence.

Solution 5.2

(a) (i) *LAST* inputs a sequence. The rule does not make sense if this sequence is empty (an empty sequence does not have a "last element"), so the domain is the set of non-empty sequences $NESEQ(X)$. The output of *LAST* is an element from the set X (whatever that might be). So the signature of *LAST* is $NESEQ(X) \longrightarrow X$.

(ii) *ADDLAST* inputs an element and a sequence, and outputs a sequence, so it has signature $X \times SEQ(X) \longrightarrow SEQ(X)$.

(In Subsection 3.2 we chose to write the input element before, rather than after, the input sequence, so the domain here is $X \times SEQ(X)$, rather than $SEQ(X) \times X$.)

You could equally well give the codomain of *ADDLAST* as $NESEQ(X)$, since its output sequence is never empty.

(b) (i) Adding 'a' to the end of an empty sequence gives the sequence $\langle \text{'a'} \rangle$.

(ii) The last element in the one-element sequence $\langle 0 \rangle$ is 0.

(iii) The empty sequence $\langle \rangle$ is not in the domain of *LAST*. So *LAST* $(\langle \rangle)$ is not defined.

Solution 5.6

(a) (i) Here $\sum s$ is

$$1 + 5 + 7 + 4 + 6 + 5 = 28.$$

(ii) Here $\sum s$ is

$$1^2 + 2^2 + 3^2 + 4^2 = 1 + 4 + 9 + 16 = 30.$$

(b) The sequence being summed is

$$\langle 1.1, 1.2, 1.3, 1.4 \rangle.$$

(The terms in the sequence are the values of $1 + 0.1m$, with $m = 1, 2, 3$ and 4.) So

$$\sum_{m=1}^{4} (1 + 0.1m) = 1.1 + 1.2 + 1.3 + 1.4 = 5.0.$$

(c) The sequence being summed is $\langle 1^3, 2^3, \ldots, 120^3 \rangle$, which can be expressed algebraically as

$$\langle n^3 : 1 \leq n \leq 120 \rangle.$$

(d) *SUM* is applied to a non-empty finite sequence of real numbers, so its domain is $NESEQ(\mathbb{R})$. Its output is a number. So *SUM* has signature $NESEQ(\mathbb{R}) \longrightarrow \mathbb{R}$.

Solution 6.3

(a) $\sin(x^2 + 5)$

(b) $\exp(3x)\sin(x^2 + 5)$

Solution 6.5

(a) A trace is given below.

memone	memtwo	memthree
x	—	—
x	$3x$	—
x	$3x - 2$	—
x	$\exp(3x - 2)$	—
x	$\exp(3x - 2)$	$5x$
x	$\exp(3x - 2)$	$\cos(5x)$
x	$\exp(3x - 2)$	$\cos(5x) \times \exp(3x - 2)$

The value calculated is $\cos(5x) \times \exp(3x - 2)$.

(b) If we collapse the right side of the tree first and then the left side, we obtain the step-by-step collapse of the tree shown in Figure S.1.

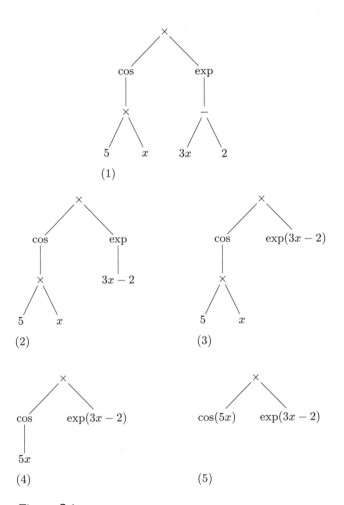

Figure S.1

Finally, we arrive at the expression represented by the tree, which is $\cos(5x)\exp(3x - 2)$. Notice how each step in the collapse matches a step in the evaluation in (a).

Solutions to Exercises

Solution 1.1

(a) To interpret this expression, you need to read:

$$\cos^3 x \text{ as } (\cos(x))^3;$$

$$2x \text{ as } 2 \times x.$$

You also need to give various evaluation precedences:

$$\cos^3 x \text{ is done before } -;$$

multiplication (in $2x$) is done before $-$.

(b) A suitable algorithm is given below.

$$\begin{aligned}
& memone := x && (1)\\
& memtwo := 2 \times memone && (2)\\
& memthree := \cos(memone) && (3)\\
& memthree := memthree^3 && (4)\\
& memtwo := memtwo - memthree && (5)
\end{aligned}$$

The calculated value is in $memtwo$.

This is not the only possible algorithm.

(c) We can trace the values taken by the variables after each step as below.

Line	memone	memtwo	memthree
1	x	$-$	$-$
2	x	$2x$	$-$
3	x	$2x$	$\cos(x)$
4	x	$2x$	$\cos^3 x$
5	x	$2x - \cos^3 x$	$\cos^3 x$

Solution 1.2

We can trace the values taken by the variables after each step as below.

Line	memone	memtwo	memthree
1	y	$-$	$-$
2	y	$y+1$	$-$
3	y	$y+1$	$y-2$
4	y	$y+1$	$(y-2)(y+1)$
5	y	$y+2$	$(y-2)(y+1)$
6	y	$y+2$	$(y+2)/((y-2)(y+1))$

The value calculated is that in $memthree$ after Line (6).

This calculation does not work for all real numbers. If y is -1 or 2, then Line (6) would involve division by zero. So these values must be excluded from the domain of the function evaluated by the algorithm. This function is

$$y \longmapsto \frac{y+2}{(y-2)(y+1)} \quad (y \text{ in } \mathbb{R},\, y \neq -1,\, y \neq 2).$$

Solution 2.1

(a) Remember that if($condition, b, c$) gives the value b when the $condition$ is true and the value c when it is false. So:

$$\text{if}(4 < 3, 7, 2) = 2 \quad (\text{since } 4 < 3 \text{ is false});$$
$$\text{if}(3 \geq 3, 5, 6) = 5 \quad (\text{since } 3 \geq 3 \text{ is true}).$$

(b) The expression if($x \geq 0, x, -x$) will give the value $|x|$, as will if($x < 0, -x, x$).

(c) (i) Substituting the given value of x in the expression $10 - 5x$ each time gives:

$$\begin{aligned}
F(0) &= \text{if}(10 \geq 0, 10, 0)\\
&= 10 \quad (\text{since } 10 \geq 0 \text{ is true});\\
F(1) &= \text{if}(5 \geq 0, 5, 0)\\
&= 5 \quad (\text{since } 5 \geq 0 \text{ is true});\\
F(3) &= \text{if}(-5 \geq 0, -5, 0)\\
&= 0 \quad (\text{since } -5 \geq 0 \text{ is false}).
\end{aligned}$$

(ii) $F(x)$ has the value $10 - 5x$, so long as $10 - 5x \geq 0$ (and this occurs so long as $x \leq 2$). Otherwise, it has the value 0. That is,

$$F(x) = \begin{cases} 10 - 5x, & \text{if } x \leq 2, \\ 0, & \text{if } x > 2. \end{cases}$$

Solution 3.1

(a) A trace is given below.

Line	screen	count
1	"boiled"	$-$
2	"boiled"	3
3	"boile"	3
4	"boile"	2
3	"boil"	2
4	"boil"	1
3	"boi"	1
4	"boi"	0

The repetition now stops, since $count = 0$ is true.

The value calculated is "boi".

(b) The algorithm deletes the last three characters from the input text. So if the text t is input, the output is the text formed by deleting the last three characters from t.

(c) Yes. The algorithm will fail if t contains less than three characters. In that case, the algorithm will attempt to apply the function $DELLAST$ to an empty piece of text, which is outside the function's domain.

(d) The algorithm evaluates a function whose domain is all pieces of text containing three or more characters. If such a piece of text t is input, then the output is formed by deleting the last three characters of t. We can take as its codomain the set of all pieces of text.

Solution 4.1

(a) $G \times H =$
$\{(\text{'a'}, 1), (\text{'a'}, 2), (\text{'b'}, 1), (\text{'b'}, 2), (\text{'c'}, 1), (\text{'c'}, 2)\}$

(b) (i) $\{n \in \mathbb{N} : 4 \leq n \leq 17\}$

(ii) $\{x \in \mathbb{R} : -6 < x^3 < 6\}$

Using the notation in (c) below, you could also write this set as

$$\{x \in \mathbb{R} : |x^3| < 6\}.$$

(c) Each of the values given in (i)–(iii) is a real number, so we just need to see whether or not it satisfies the given condition.

(i) $|1 - 3| = |-2| = 2$, which *is* less than 5.

(ii) $|10 - 3| = |7| = 7$, which is *not* less than 5.

(iii) $|7.32 - 3| = |4.32| = 4.32$, which *is* less than 5.

So the numbers in (i) and (iii) *are* in A, but that in (ii) is not in A. Thus (i) and (iii) are true, but (ii) is false.

Solution 4.2

(a) The character c is a lower-case letter if its ASCII code lies between the values 97 and 122 inclusive. So the condition may be expressed as

$$(97 \leq ASC(c)) \; AND \; (ASC(c) \leq 122).$$

(b) This condition may be expressed as

$$NOT((x = 0) \; AND \; (y = 0)).$$

Note that this condition is false when $x = 0$ and $y = 0$, but is true when, for example, $x = 0$ and $y = 1$. It is a *different* condition from

$$(NOT(x = 0)) \; AND \; (NOT(y = 0))$$

(note the different positioning of the brackets) which would be false in both cases.

Solution 5.1

(a) You can use a similar structure to the algorithm in Activity 5.4. This time, though, you need to use *memone* to store the accumulated total of the numbers in the sequence. Each number in the sequence s should be added to *memone*, in turn, then deleted from the sequence in *memtwo*. To achieve this, you need to modify only Line (3). This gives the following algorithm.

Set *memone* equal to 0.	(1)
Set *memtwo* equal to s.	(2)
Repeat the instructions:	
add the last number in *memtwo* to the value in *memone*;	(3)
delete the last number from the sequence in *memtwo*;	(4)
until the sequence in *memtwo* is empty.	
The calculated value is in *memone*.	

The first line in the algorithm in Activity 5.4 is not needed here, since you know from the question that s cannot be empty.

This algorithm is expressed algebraically below.

$memone := 0$
$memtwo := s$
Repeat the instructions:
   $memone := memone + LAST(memtwo)$
   $memtwo := DELLAST(memtwo)$
until $ISEMPTY(memtwo)$.
The calculated value is in *memone*.

(b) If $s = \langle 2, 3, 5 \rangle$ is input, we can trace the algorithm as follows.

Line	*memone*	*memtwo*
1	0	–
2	0	$\langle 2, 3, 5 \rangle$
3	5	$\langle 2, 3, 5 \rangle$
4	5	$\langle 2, 3 \rangle$
3	8	$\langle 2, 3 \rangle$
4	8	$\langle 2 \rangle$
3	10	$\langle 2 \rangle$
4	10	$\langle \rangle$

The value calculated is the final value in *memone*, which is 10.

The algorithm is intended to calculate $\sum s$. With $s = \langle 2, 3, 5 \rangle$,

$$\sum s = 2 + 3 + 5 = 10.$$

So the algorithm has calculated the correct value in this case.